THE MOMENT I SHOULD HAVE BOUNCED

Raymond W.S Brown

The Moment I Should Have Bounced
Copyright © 2021 by Raymond W.S Brown

All rights reserved. No part of this book may be reproduced or transmitted in any form or by any means, electronic or mechanical, including photocopying, recording, or by any information storage and retrieval system, without permission in writing from the copyright owner.

This is a work of fiction. Names, characters, places and incidents either are the product of the author's imagination or are used fictitiously, and any resemblance to any actual persons, living or dead, events, or locales is entirely coincidental.

Library of Congress Control Number: 2021911544
ISBN-13:   Paperback: 978-1-64749-440-7
          ePub: 978-1-64749-441-4

Printed in the United States of America

GoToPublish LLC
1-888-337-1724
www.gotopublish.com
info@gotopublish.com
TMISHB@yahoo.com

CONTENTS

Dedication v
Forward vi
Bounce 1 1
Bounce 2 5
Bounce 3 8
Bounce 4 11
Bounce 5 13
Bounce 6 15
Bounce 7 20
Bounce 8 24
Bounce 9 26
Bounce 10 32
Bounce 11 35
Bounce 12 38
Bounce 13 40
Bounce 14 43
Bounce 15 45
Bounce 16 49
Bounce 17 52
Bounce 18 55
Bounce 19 58
Bounce 20 63
Bounce 21 68
Bounce 22 71
Bounce 23 74
Bounce 24 76
Bounce 25 78
Bounce 26 80
Bounce 27 83
Bounce 28 85
Bounce 29 87

Bounce 30 88
Bounce 31 89
Bounce 32 91
Bounce 33 93
Bounce 34 95
Bounce 35 97
Bounce 36 99
Bounce 37 102
Bounce 38 104
Bounce 39 107
Bounce 40 114

DEDICATION

I dedicate this book to the memory of Grandmother to whom I owe everything. She raised me to respect god, myself, and others. I would not be able to do anything without her love, guidance, and of course the beatings of my life. She cared when no one else in my family thought about raising me and my brother. I was fortunate to have her in my life early and spent precious time with her before she passed on to heaven. I love and miss her presence tremendously.

FORWARD

I'm writing this book for all the people that suffered through relationships and looked back and thought on the single most qualifying moment in the relationship when they should have made the decision to leave without any regrets. After talking to several groups of people men and women and using my own experiences from my various encounters. I finally sat down one day and thought about my unfulfilled relationships throughout my short life. I kept thinking about how and when things went wrong during the course of those courtships. Every time I heard about someone breaking up or separating it was a similar theme that a certain important Point in the relationship was ignored for love, money, lies, pregnancy, or false hopes of success between the two individuals.

Collectively this formed. I know people like to hang in there and try and work things out but sometimes one must be honest with the other and themselves, which is difficult for many people.

The worst case scenario is trying or believing one will change and the situation turns into domestic violence. We see it time and time again on the news someone missing or dead and the family is saying we told them usually a female to leave that person alone. Men also go through it with some relationships. Once you recognize your moment to bounce a lot of grief and misfortune at the hands of another could be avoided. I know drama comes with relationships but too much drama early in a relationship is truly the moment to bounce.

BOUNCE 1

As I step back down memory lane one of my first lasting experiences that seemed like a tour of duty in the armed services why you ask because I was always on guard. This story led me to start my journey to writing this book. I met this girl at a job function and we hit it off after a few dances. She was beautiful and had a nice smile. I drove her home that night and we made plans to go on a date. One date led to another and we became joined as a couple. She had no children, lived in a room and was carefree so to speak I mean available with what seemed no hang ups. Of course as the relationship moved on a few snags occurred but like any other person on the road to love we tend to overlook what we consider less menial things. I'm not saying everything that happens in a relationship needs to be addressed but it seems if these things are not clarified they can be interpreted incorrectly by either party. The incident that stands out in my mind was the day we returned from buying food at a local restaurant. We went back to her house to eat and of course enjoy one another's company.

We consumed our meal with brief discussion and later got cleaned up after our passionate time together. I'm not sure why I decided to leave that night but I kissed her good night and proceeded home.

The neighborhood she lived in was known for car theft and vandalism and I guess that was in the back of my mind somewhere and made the thought of leaving my car parked overnight uncomfortable. I drove home happy and content without any complaints listening to the overnight radio station blurt out love songs. I find when one's in a seemingly satisfying relationship love songs seem to play on the radio one after the other.

Once I arrived home I called her to let her know I arrived home safe and hearing her say goodnight before I went to sleep you know the last voice one hears.

The next morning I awoke it was Sunday and I was off from work. When one has a woman, men learn not to make plans until you hear from your other half. So like a good soldier I waited to hear from her but by noon I had not heard a peep. I called her around 1pm after I'd shower eaten breakfast, lunch, watched some sports and relaxed a little. I was very surprised when she did not answer the phone so I left a message. A few more hours went by and I started to wonder what was going on. I hung out with some friends and returned to the crib and still no call or message on the home phone.

I ironed my things for the next work day and finally was ready for bed. It must have been eleven thirty at night when my phone finally rang.

It was the young lady I waited to hear from all day who finally decided to call. I asked her why she did not return my call and she said she was in the emergency room all day possibly sick from the food we consumed the day before. I let her talk on and on until finally she stopped and noticed I was not saying anything. She asked me what's wrong. Why are you not talking? I told her sometimes it's just good to listen.

I was never satisfied with her explanation as to why she did not call her man who incidentally ate the same food to see if I felt sick from the food. Instead I got this unrealistic not well thought out excuse that made me want to never call her again but I remained.

When she stopped the conversation noting I was not buying it at all I should have made a decision to bounce at that moment.

I thought to myself I know she was not in no hospital and did not call me once. Those of you thinking did I ask her why she didn't call of course I did. Her answer was she did not want to bother me. What kind of lame ass answer was that to give your man, needless to say we broke up that same night during that same conversation.

She used that as her moment to bounce stating she was not the girl for me and proceeded to tell me what type of woman I needed

She made it clear she was not the one for me. A clear clue she had already moved on. I saw her again not too long after we broke up with her new man while getting my hair cut. The dude she was with actually tried to shake my hand as if to say no hard feelings. I declined the handshake because it was not necessary and I did not know him. Karma has a way of biting one in the ass so hard it makes you cry. I received a call from her. I'm not sure how long after but she told me how her new love almost killed her or rather the guy in the relationship with her almost killed her. It seems the dude, unlike me, was insanely jealous and he wanted to twitter her meaning he wanted to know every step she took from the time her eyes opened to the time they closed. It seems he tried to break down her door, stalk her, and anything else involving keeping tabs on her. She had to get a restraining order for him to finally leave her alone. This was one of those rare times the restraining order worked. I had to of course put my two cents in stating, "If you would have stayed with me that would not have happened" as I chuckled in disbelief about the entire situation. Prior to all of this I asked this woman to marry me in a restaurant and she hesitated. That was my moment to bounce but I did not.

Today looking back I'm sure I really loved her and I did not want anyone else to have her. Once we broke up I realized how heavy she was and how tired I was of carrying her all the time. The saying he's not heavy he's my brother did not apply. She was heavy. Looking back it was certain things she did not do in a relationship that others did or tried to do. She never once offered to pay for anything or go half I mean at least make the offer you know fake reach for the check knowing full well if dude is worth anything he is not going to let you pay. Ladies this only works if the guy is interested in you further than a friendship.

Note to self and reader It is nothing wrong with taking your woman out and treating her like a queen but that is under the pretense a future can be seen with this person. If either party has any reservations about the future of their relationship comes into play don't fool yourself, be honest and accept or release the individual or disaster will follow. Once she realized her interest in me waned I wish she would have ended it with me. I'm grown, I can handle being rejected. Although we remain in contact mainly through social media as friends I managed to put this behind me.

I ran into a dude not too long after she shared her story with me at the very same barber shop where we were introduced. In her conversation with me she added if I see him he may try and tell me some lies about her. To my surprise he began to tell me she was cheating on me. I suspected she was cheating. I'm no dummy. I stopped him in his tracks and said

"Whatever happened before or after you two I don't want to hear it" and walked away. I call what he was doing a real bitch move.

BOUNCE 2

My next encounter led me to this woman I instantly fell for not because she was drop dead gorgeous and she was but her personality was down to earth. I was immediately attracted to her and I suspect she was to me to a degree but I had to really rap my ass off to get with her. I played it cool the first time we met and did not come on to her right away.

She had a small child about 2-3 years old. We started to speak more and more each day until finally we went on a date and had a very nice time you know the regular dinner and movie and polite conversation which turned into a sex conversation between two adults but I steered it back to her being alone with a child. I like to know what I'm getting into before I take that leap of faith.

This story takes a rather bizarre twist because we would see each other every chance we got but it was for short periods of time. One evening we were to get together and when she did not show up I called her and her child answered the phone.

I asked to speak with the mother and the daughter said she doesn't want to speak to you and hung up the phone. I called back of course thinking the child was playing but on the next call I heard the mother telling the child what to say to me over the phone. A 3 year old being forced to give messages to an adult.

I finally convinced her to get on the phone and speak directly to me only to find out she was drunk. I had no clue she drank to the point she had no recollection of speaking to me the next day. I'd heard of blackouts but never witnessed one until now because of my prior relationship involving substance abuse. She managed to take a cab to the house with her child in tow. When she arrived she smelled like a liquor store but I took her in anyway. I mean this chick was torn up or as we say in the hood tore-up from the floor up. The next morning when she awoke she did not realize she had come to my home.

After she showered and got cleaned up I got her to eat something so we could clear the air once and for all. I asked her if she was upset about something I did. She answered no so I recalled the conversation from the night before and she seemed like she remembered bits and pieces so I filled in the blanks. I found out why she was acting the way she did. apparently she was not pleased with her daughter sleeping on the pull out couch in the living room while we slept in the bedroom.

I realized at that point I should have bounced because she had a problem with drugs and communication especially over something so petty or I should have shown her the door but of course I let my heart do the talking instead of listening to my head. Eventually we went our separate ways.

Looking back at that moment in time I should have ended that terrible union after I realized she had a serious drinking problem that she never got any help and refused to believe she had a problem. I pulled up in my car at a bus stop after noticing her waiting on the bus. This is now about 4 years later and she looked well and told me she was involved with an older guy. We spoke about the good ole days but after a while she noticed and made note to me her bus was coming unless I was going to give her a ride. I responded with let me let you go and drove away.

I would have offered her a ride but did not want to send mixed messages. I was polite but knew our time had ended and it was no use keeping in touch with her for any reason did I mention I can see the future. I'm no psychic but during any conversation once can discern what is about to happen if they pay close attention.

Note to self and reader I have come to understand in these different experiences I played a major role in how my moment to bounce opinion is formed. I never looked for a reason to dismiss anyone but everyone should have a certain set of standards to live and abide no matter what the circumstances surrounding the situation. The difficult part is recognizing your moment and being willing to effect the change in one's life. This is where love makes things very confusing but as I always say it's great to be in love but never lose track of reality.

BOUNCE 3

I was seeing this next young lady for about a month and I really started forming feelings of love for her. I mean in my eyes she was the one I was falling in love with to the point we would have gotten married, kids, and the whole nine yards. We met at her job and it took me a few weeks but finally we started dating. I was actually interested in another girl at her job but found out she was moving out of state soon. I then turned my attention to her and the rest they say is history. We went to movies, plays, pool, bowling, you know, spent a lot of time together even horseback riding.

We returned to my home after a beautiful night out to make love for the first time we fooled around before but never to what we were going to do that night.

I believe I was unhooking her bra and the phone rang. Now most people would have ignored the phone and continued on with what they were doing.

 If you understand me then you know why I answered the phone. I'm of the belief if one has nothing to hide it is perfectly ok to answer the phone. Looking back if I had it to do again that phone would have rung off the hook. It was a woman friend one I'd had no sexual dealings with at that point in time. When I told her I had company and would talk to her later she became very persistent in trying to keep me on the phone I never guessed she had a thing for me. I hung up the phone and this fool called back and began questioning me about who I was and what's her name. I became very annoyed and stated loud enough for my date to hear "what is wrong with you we are not dating nor have we ever so I owe you no explanation". I again hung up this chick and kept calling at this point she became a real bird. The young lady I was so crazy about said to me after promptly putting her shirt back on "take me home".

I explained to her this girl and I had nothing going on and she was acting stupid. My date's response shocked me. I really didn't expect her to say what she said I admit the phone nut was someone

I'd pursued in the past but nothing came of it and of all nights to use my number she picked that night and messed up my future.

Don't get me wrong I was really feeling this girl to the point of having a future. That one phone call I believe changed the course of my life. That's how serious I was about this woman. The young lady said to me she must have some feelings for you if she is acting like that and I want no parts of it. That was her moment to bounce and she did.

I did not understand it at first but she did not want any drama in her life and did not need to get involved with anyone that has a possible lunatic attached to them. I respect her decision today back then and I of course did not see her point. I called her but she never returned my calls.

I ran into her some time later and we went out again a few times I thought we could rekindle what we lost but the spark was gone. She told me after she and I stop dating she met and started dating a guy that smoked those nasty cigarettes, had a child, drank beer excessively, and had a propensity to become violent. I was surprised when she told me her family would ask where was I and she never responded to them because her new boyfriend would get angry at the mention of my name. I'm sure she mentioned to him some of the things we did which may have caused him to get a little jealous.

I'm of the belief in some cases beyond one's control a second chance can be given like the one I was granted. After she told me about the guy I would be following I was honestly turned off.

I figured if you settled for someone that smoked, had a child from a previous relationship which means you had to deal with possible baby mama drama and when he drinks he's on the brink of becoming physically abusive to you but you became bent out of shape over a phone call from someone I had no dealings with at all.

After hearing about the guy she dated, that was my moment to bounce but I did not have to. we lost contact and I've never heard from her again. Don't get me wrong it's nothing wrong with dating someone with children but from what she told me dude was not a totally responsible father.

Note to self and readers a flaw among people who are dating whether exclusive or just having fun is they go way overboard when the other person is just not that interested to the same point they are in the relationship. This was something I was guilty of which helped to create the moment to bounce.

BOUNCE 4

Let's visit a couple I know were married and met in college and had kids the so called American dream. Somewhere in their relationship things took a turn and they stopped enjoying one another's company and started seeking the company of others throughout the entire courtship. They were exclusive and genuinely interested in one another after the children were when things went downhill well not right after but say after the last child was born.

The main problem that was nagging to him was his wife developed this condition which is known as narcolepsy. That's the inability to stay awake under your own power. These bouts of narcolepsy occurred during disagreements and of course love making. Although he never considered this a reason or moment to bounce from his family it was certainly suspect during the entire time they dated she never once had this problem and usually these things manifest themselves long before your late adulthood. I'm in no way taking sides because I don't have all the information meaning both sides of the story as the saying goes there is his side, her side and the truth. Needless to say their end result was divorce. Thinking back my friend would have bounced a long time ago when she refused to keep the house clean of pet crap if no children were involved. Who wants to come home to animal shit all over the house?

Another time he caught her lying about seeing someone and they eventually worked it out with the help of a mediator. It still did not change the fact that throughout this ordeal I'm sure the both of them shared thought.

While it's difficult to see things for what they are when you're in love or think you are, I've always said never lose track of reality. Instead of the both of them talking about the issues bothering them or what concerned each of them in their marriage. They decided to find solace in the arms of others. In this case they stayed together for the children, another mistake couples make all too often.

Note to self and reader almost too often the art of conversation is absent and ignorance and anger take over when a couple stop talking and fall out of love. Once a point is reached during the relationship that leads you to considering cheating on your significant other it is time for professional help or one of you to bounce. Another interesting experience not necessarily my own but it involved me to a degree. Listening to people spill their guts about personal experiences takes a degree of skill. One needs to know how to decipher truth from bullshit. Often this is handed to me when I ask them about that one moment they should have bounced.

BOUNCE 5

I asked a female friend to give me some insight on her failed relationships and at what moment she felt she should have bounced before she invested too much of herself.

She informed me she usually is the one that gets dropped except for this one time when she became involved with a guy that clearly told her he did not want a relationship because he was pursing school and personal goals but would readily satisfy her primal urges for sex.

This young lady is in full command of the English language and understood fully when the guy told her clearly he does not want a relationship yet she still slept with him thinking he may change his mind after he gets a taste of her love cipher.

Needless to say he stuck to his guns and was honest with her from the beginning. She of course did not take him seriously and after a couple more romps in the sack she decided this was her moment to bounce because the situation is not going to change. I also found out she was always the one to initiate contact with him.

Here is some background information about this woman I neglected to consider in this story. She for some reason had a thing for married men or men in current relationships. Once she and I shared a phone conversation concerning a new love of mine I was considering marrying.

I have always been up front about having a girl if I met someone and we were talking and the subject came up. The next thing she said caught me off guard near the end of the conversation she said let me know if things don't work out between you and your girl maybe we can get together. Knowing this woman's track record and how she let men treat her like trash I never considered anything of the kind.

Note to self and reader although one may be attracted to someone's goal spirit an important element to consider when it comes to dealing in the real world.

If a guy or girl isn't willing to make time for you to pursue a relationship or tells you they don't want what you want. Leave that type of dude or female alone they are doing more than what's being revealed to you. If they can make time for sex they can make time for other things and they do just not with you. They could not possibly be busy every second of the day. People often think women can change this kind of behavior like a science project.

BOUNCE 6

This next young lady I met was very nice, great looking and fresh out the hospital. I have always been busy working and going to school so I took to the internet to find that special someone.

We met at a public restaurant after talking a few times and hit it off right away but I noticed she kept leaning to the left.

I asked her if she was ok and she informed me she had surgery a week ago and the stitches just broke. I of course wanted to know why you are out here if you should be home resting or on your way to the hospital. She later admitted the stitches had broken a day ago and she did not want to return to the emergency room. We could have postponed this date until you healed.

I wasn't too concerned but kept that information in the corner of my mind. It later made me think of several possibilities about how she lives her life. One she is lazy and does not want to take care of herself and two she did not take her health seriously. I looked at it and it was infected. I believe I gave her bacitracin antibiotic ointment to put on it and advised her to clean it with peroxide.

Anyway she and I got along well starting seeing one another and spent a lot of our after work time at my place. I learned she did not eat vegetables or beans. This explained why her healing after surgery was taking so long. It also confirmed what I thought about her not caring about her health. I liked this girl but after learning more about her she started to become less attractive to me. I believe like everyone else, give the person a chance they may change. Everything was going great until one day she took her car to have the transmission oil change

THE MOMENT I SHOULD HAVE BOUNCED

The transmission place failed to inform her sometimes when they change very old transmission fluid on a very old car the transmission may not work correctly. She called me from the service facility upset about her car not driving correctly after the fluid was changed. I told her to take it back and have them correct what they messed up. After the second day I happened to be off from work and went down there with her to find out what was preventing them from fixing her car. While we waited on a bench for them to start work a mechanic walked by us and said to her "how are you today baby."

What was more shocking than him saying what he said in my presence? She had the nerve to answer this fool with a smile on her face? It took me a moment to get over the initial shock of this idiot trying to commit suicide and her with him.

I asked him whom are you talking to because I did not see anyone that resembled a baby. She tried to defend this fool saying oh he didn't mean anything we have been joking around since he's seen me here several days. I asked her was she crazy or stupid I exploded me and dude almost came to blows. The mechanics boss heard all the commotion and came out of his office and asked what's going on. I asked him if your mechanic called your wife who happened to be sitting in the office baby. He answered no and I explained the situation he spoke with the mechanic showing him the error of his ways. After all that was done I turned to her and asked why you let this man to call you baby and you responded like it was ok.

She exclaimed I don't want to argue about it! That was my moment but of course I became angry and told her since you enjoyed that so much let him bring you home and bounced.

When she arrived home she still did not want to discuss it any further so I let it go wrong. If it were any reason to bounce that was it. The fact that she did not want to discuss this even at home should have made me end it on the spot. I cared for her and wanted to try and make this work. I was tired of going from relationship to relationship.

So I ignored the obvious and did not pursue any further discussion that would have definitely turned into an argument. I let it go and that I'm certain created our moment without a doubt.

That just set the scene for her dismissal. Weeks passed and her birthday arrived and I surprised her with a new car. She could not believe it but it was hers her credit was jacked so I had to put it in my name all she had to do was make the payments.

Ordinarily I would not do anything like that but I loved her and she needed a new car badly. A few months passed and we were doing well. She was enjoying her new car by this time she had moved in with me.

I was home watching television on a Saturday after I returned home from work when she arrived home from school. We had no plans and I was working weekends at this particular job.

No sooner than she stepped through the door her cell rang and she was refusing an invitation to a party loud enough for me to hear. When she got off the phone she protested a bit too much for someone not wanting to go to the party. Then about thirty minutes later she proclaimed how tired she was but because dude she was on the phone with a lot of people on her side job it would be good for her to meet these people.

She decided to go for a little while. She never once asked me if I wanted to hang out or go to the party.

After she showered and changed and was about to leave an invitation was extended to me. I declined and she was gone in sixty seconds saying I will not be out long that was around eight o'clock at night.

As far as I know when someone says they will not stay long it means two-three hours I could be wrong.

I fell asleep on the couch and woke up about eleven thirty which means she'd been gone about three and a half hours. I got ready for bed

THE MOMENT I SHOULD HAVE BOUNCED

thinking she will be in shortly besides I had to work the next morning I went to bed. I awoke the next morning the only one in bed. I thought maybe she slept on the couch not to wake me to my surprise. I was scheduled to arrive at work at seven am. I arrived at work on time and began to set up for my morning medication distribution. I received a call from her at approximately nine-thirty in the middle of me giving out medication.

She asked me what's going on. I responded that I'm a little busy. We will talk when I get home and we hang up. She called me again about an hour later to inform me she was going shopping and was there anything special I wanted for dinner. I said no and again told her we would talk later this was her way of trying to gauge my attitude.

Folks reading this you and I know she messed up right. I arrived home and she was asleep. I turned on the television and she emerged from the bedroom a short time later. I turned off the T.V. and asked her if we could talk. I started by saying this last incident left a bad taste in my mouth.

She could not understand why I had a problem with her staying out all night with a male friend. She explained to me they were up talking all night then she fell asleep on his couch. I guess that was supposed to make me feel better. I asked her what time she came home. She of course knew she had to tell me a little after seven. She claimed she had too much to drink and didn't feel comfortable driving back home we now shared as a couple. I wanted to know why continue to drink knowing you did not plan on being out late.

Since your judgment was impaired to the point you could not drive what other bad decisions did you make that evening besides not coming home or calling me to pick you up. She had no answer to that but nonetheless I ended our union and asked her to move out; she complied with my request. That was my moment to bounce and I exercised every bit of it.

I should have seen it coming when she was too comfortable with the mechanic that called her baby. She had to make him become very comfortable for him to think that was alright and did not mention she had a man. Ladies and men make it really clear to other men and women especially if you're involved with someone you care about. It is not cool for another man or woman to try and get slick at the mouth and you condone it.

Note to self reader no one in a relationship should go against the other unless you're ready to end the relationship. That really shows lack of respect for your relationship to allow another man to call you any other name but your own. It should not matter if your man or woman is around or not.

I have never experienced my woman ever putting me in a situation like that not even as a teenager. It's funny how things start to come together as I think about how it went down. I'm not saying something happened the night she spent out but ladies if your living with your man and he's cool with you having male friends especially those that were in your life before he arrived have sense enough to know no man or woman in their right mind I know is going to be okay with his women or her man staying out all night under no circumstances.

BOUNCE 7

My next experience I thought would last but turned into a shaky stormy romance that was great until of course an event changed our course. I met her believe it or not through the kiss fm hookup line. She left me a message

I returned her call and we eventually left our respective contact numbers because this radio station was for the grown and mature.

We spoke quite frequently and I was nothing short of a gentleman the first time we felt comfortable enough to meet and go out. She was so cute I could not understand why she was single. I later found out she was indeed separated and had a small child. I met the child, very nice and polite, a little shy but still friendly. I would bring a gift for the child each visit and would leave the gift if the child was with dad that weekend.

We spent a lot of quality time together because I was working two jobs and whatever time I had I would travel to see her. She even offered to chip in on the gas and toll.

I didn't think it was fair to ask her to do the traveling because she had the child with her and did not have a car at the time.

Note to self and reader never stop someone willing to make a personal sacrifice for you. I said that because I was always willing to make it easier for the person in my experiences but never stopped to think maybe this person feels the same way I do about sacrificing for someone they care about on the way to love.

Let's continue the story on why she and I did not make it. I helped her move one weekend and the new place was a nice size. She asked me to move in with her after we dated for a while

She wanted me to quit my job and move to another borough and start over from a job I'd been on for approximately eight years.

I really did not see the benefit in leaving my apartment and job at the time to move into her home. We had not been dating over six months when she asked me to move in with her. I've been taught living with someone before marriage was a mistake and when I strayed from my beliefs it always ended in disaster. I was not willing to do that just yet although we had quality time together. I believe when I declined to move in with her that started the downward spiral for us.

Then we almost overnight did not see each other as much. One evening when I was at her home she told me she had something to discuss with me I did not know what to expect. She told me she had a miscarriage that's why she was acting kind of distant. I asked her if it was me and she flipped out. I explained to her we were in a different space and I was not sure what was going on so I'm one to ask questions straight no chaser I wanted to know. Often men do not ask enough questions and get caught out there.

She announced to me after our discussion we would no longer be intimate and I informed her I did not sign up for that kind of relationship and if that's the deal I'm out. I exercised my moment to bounce.

Today in hindsight I acted too quickly without thinking I would agree but you can't start something one way and then mid stream change the rules because you did not like what was said.

I did not bounce immediately because she was a rational intelligent woman but I'd breached her trust by saying those three words no woman likes to hear. I knew once she made a decision like that she would keep her word. I should have been done but I hung in there to answer your question. I loved her that's why. It was not my intention to bounce at the time but she was acting funky towards me without any explanation. The visits became far and few between and eventually we drifted apart.

We reconnected and went out and tried to get it back on track but the only thing I did was waste time and money. We eventually fizzed out again.

Note to self and reader women do it all the time they stay in these loveless relationships thinking it will change. I was no different. She called me again after several years later only to learn I'd gotten married. She later admitted to me she was jealous that I moved on and was happy at least when I spoke to her at that particular time. I will discuss my defunct marriage time later in the book. She said she dated after us but it was not the same. I agreed and did not know why but I did. My wife and I were separated but not completely over at this point and I had no intentions on cheating. This woman was not the type to take advantage of another woman especially if she knows it's a possibility of them getting back together. Oh yes I was married for a short time more to follow on that matter. We had lunch, talked over old times, laughed and cleared the air and caught up. I believe she called me to ask a question about diabetes and drinking. A family member of hers was in trouble from doing some serious lifetime drinking and was now paying for it medically. I explained diabetes to her and the conversation shifted because now I was single again. She had strange habits not impossible to deal with but I could not deal with the same things that irritated me about her. They remained except now she was in a new apartment. When I came to visit her she gave me directions. I asked for the address because I have a GPS. She said she did not know her address and still uses a P.O. Box. How does a woman of a certain age not know the address to where they reside. I made it through her directions and the help of Popeye's chicken.

None the less the last time we encountered one another I suggested we spend the weekend together you would have thought I cursed at her or called her out her name. I never heard from her again. Sadly enough

I do miss her because I feel we really did not get to know one another long enough to accomplish anything.

BOUNCE 8

My next experience is with a young lady I met while training to change my career from selling chicken to the medical profession. I was in for a big surprise with this woman. We attended a training school together and graduated without a problem.

The entire time we were in class I did not pay too much attention to her. I was working on another lady but it turned out she had a baby by a dude that didn't care about her and as the story goes she was still in love with a no good baby daddy.

Near the end of the course ole girl I paid no attention to we started talking and low and behold she was really cool. She always had a smile on her face and seemed genuinely happy. As always everything is not as it seems on the surface she had a dark side.

After learning the information I'm about to share I'm not sure how she got through the course. We graduated and started seeing one another after a night of celebration drinking included.

I dropped her off one day at her mom's home and did not hear from her for several days. I went to the house she was not home. Her mom sat me down and started to unravel a tale of how her daughter was an addict for a long time complete with disappearing acts and rehabs.

I had no idea she had a problem with anything she hid it well. This was my first introduction to substance abuse. That was my moment to bounce but I stayed and I was determined to help this girl through this. Let's face it I have a kind heart. I stuck in there and put up with as much as possible until I could not take it. I even considered letting her stay in the crib and do drugs.

That was the craziest thought I've ever had but its said love makes one do crazy things. That did not work either since she was the only one getting high. This time when she disappeared I changed the locks and put her out.

We reconnected as friends she claimed she was off the drugs and from what I could see she was clean. She even had her son with her now and I really believed she was ok at least for now.

She did a lot of amazing work on herself and to this day is doing well. I guess when you're ready to put the drugs down eventually it will happen but it's up to the individual.

Note to self and reader It is important to know what ones are getting into and to keep your eyes open. Disappearing is not part of a relationship and should be addressed if it arises. Ask questions pry if you really care and love this person it could save you time and grief.

BOUNCE 9

We now get into my next experience of the love I lost was a sweet love. We met before we met meaning I kept hearing about this girl how fine she was. I remember I was eating my lunch in the lounge and happened to look up and saw this beautiful girl staring. I'm not sure she was looking at me or the food. I offered her a piece of my golden brown succulent chicken..

She claimed I made it look so good but after she tasted it she knew the deal. After we became acquainted I would prepare extra food because we now shared lunch and dialogue between one another and oh lord the bullshit started on the job.

This poor girl had to endure some of the cruelest shit because she paid me some attention and the other cats that stepped to her got no play. We became friends quickly and other women on the job tried to approach me but they were not suave about it at all.

One chick called the extension I was sitting at and asked me "what are we doing tonight" I said nothing and hung up.

She called back and was irate that I hung up on her weak proposal. I explained to her do not approach me under cloak and dagger if you want to speak to me in person.

She could not understand why I turned down what I call an easy ass. That's right ladies when you call a man you do not know asking what are we doing tonight your easy ass. I've never been partial to easy ass no matter what the situation.

The young lady in question was nothing like that; she was down to earth friendly and most of all smart. She conducted herself like a lady and never had to front for others. When we started having lunch the place seemed like it focused on us only.

A married female coworker asked me why I did not bring her lunch. Of course I looked at her like she was crazy and replied ask your husband to make you lunch. This was how insane this situation had become at work. One day she approached me and said she needed a favor and would ask me during lunch. All day I wondered what she wanted finally it was lunch time. I set out our spread and we began to talk.

She unraveled a story of her mom's money mismanagement that resulted in her asking me to loan her three hundred dollars to help pay the electric bill. I of course gave her the money without a second thought. I always believe in helping other people whenever I could if I had the means. I never placed money in such high regard that I would not help a friend.

Besides whenever I loan money I never look for it back so if I do get it cool if not no love loss. It also helped that I liked her a lot and she shared very personal details of her life with me that she did not have too. She told me she felt very comfortable talking to me and trusted me for some unknown reason. I guess because I was not salivating all over her or trying to screw her every chance I got she appreciated our friendship and it continued to grow.

One evening she asked me for a ride to the train station now usually her kids father would pick her up but lately those rides were far and few between. I learned through our conversations they did everything but break up which was coming soon.

One day she started to tell me her story of betrayal and deceit and I shared my failed marriage tale of woe. We laughed and shared food and looked into each other's eyes gazing wide eyed. We started to spend a lot of friendship time together way before we started dating. We took a couple of trips and had a very good time as we grew closer.

We eventually spent so much time together that people thought we were a couple. I finally asked her to be my lady and she did not accept right away and asked could she think about it.

She eventually accepted and I was happier than I'd been in a long time. I also got to know her children during our courtship not as much as I'd liked but they were very polite and mannerly.

As I think back I realized she never really let me have that much exposure to the kids except when we went to her house. I figured since I was spending money on them something their father was doing very little of I should spend more time with them or we should have spent more time with them because if we were planning a future together and she was willing to have another child for me it would have been a perfect opportunity to see me in action did I mention kids love me.

Things are never the way we plan them and I believe god has a plan for all of us. She has met my grandmother and some of my family when we took a trip south. I like the women in my life not to be dependent on me because one never knows what can happen. She kind of had an idea of how to drive and was pretty good but I made sure she practiced every opportunity she had because I refuse to chauffer anyone around except my grandmother.

Once she was proficient in driving I would stupidly on my part allow her to use my car while I was in school with only her permit again love makes one do silly stupid things.

One day she picked me and a good friend of mine up after school the front bumper of the truck was twisted. She hit a train pillar trying to turn and avoid another car. I did not get upset until it cost me five bills to have it fixed. I paid cash that pissed me off. The car was a lease.

After that I took the car for a minute until she got her license. I let her use that car and I got another for myself. It seemed everything was coming together after the second year I asked her to marry me and gave her a ring

It was great I was in love again and thought she was the one. Until one day we were at my home it seems she was not getting my text during the week. She was in the shower and I decided to test her phone out to see if it were a problem with my phone or hers not receiving the text messages.

I texted her and nothing happened. I did not know her phone was on silent not vibrate silent. I picked up the phone to check the message and I read something from someone I could only assume was her second boyfriend. All I remember was becoming very warm and angry all at once. When I get angry my voice becomes very deep and I'm told I get this scowl on my face.

I managed to control myself and when she stepped into the room I asked her who is texting you. They miss you and you return the text of how you miss them too. She of course tried to flip it and said "why are you checking my messages."

I explained to her what I was doing and why with no intentions of spying on her. She told me this was someone she knew but they meant nothing of course everyone is thinking this should have been my moment to bounce but no it was not.

I was ready to bounce but she cried and didn't want me to leave her although I had every text message reason to leave.

We worked through it like two adults she claimed she never cheated on me with him or anyone else. She'd never to my knowledge cheated on me or lied to me so I was inclined to believe her or I convinced myself to swallow that bullshit. Shortly after that she called me in a panic saying she had something to tell me but didn't know how. I replied" just say it".

It seems she took her engagement ring off for whatever reason and thought she placed it on her table but noticed she could not find it.

She finally remembered it was in her purse and after she had the car washed and vacuumed is when she could not find it.

That is the true moment I should have bounced. We continued on with our relationship but as life has it another milestone came up. It seems her sister was getting married and I could not go because there were too many people so she trimmed some from the roster. My fiancé said she would not go if I was not invited. I told her listen that's your sister and you're in the wedding don't worry about me I'll be ok. They all went on the wedding/ honeymoon/cruise. When she returned she was very distant and we had not spent any time together since her return.

Finally she came over to the house. Remember I said previously we had not spent any real time together in a while so I was horny as hell. I stayed horny because we broke up so she broke up with me and broke my heart in half.

I was not bitter and she claimed she was not leaving me for another person. She told me this story and made me promise I would never repeat it and I kept my promise. We stayed friends till this day although since our relationship ended she went on to have another child. She has since admitted to me she made a mistake leaving and restated to me she was going through something at the time.

Note to self and reader we all go through something but isn't the point of having someone to count on is to lean on them during that emotional time of need.

Too many people, men and women make the mistake of taking off and running instead of dealing with their issues. If we tried to work on the problem and the result was us separating then at least a solution was attempted. As we talked she claimed she realized she was still in love with me and because of this I think in this case she now sees the grass is not always greener as so many that dealt with me soon learn. I'm not one to give everyone a second chance. When we speak to one another and breach the subject of us and she claims she made a mistake and realized she was still in love with me making it difficult for her to move on although she now has two more kids then when we met I'd say she has moved on in a way. My question is once she realized she was still in love with me why didn't you come back to me. I of course never got a straight answer.

BOUNCE 10

Another woman I experienced was rather weird in our dealings only because she was still catering to her son's father who incidentally was doing nothing to help her situation just making things more difficult. We spoke about how she was making things too convenient for him but she had to be the uncomfortable one. Clearly she had low self esteem issues.

She demonstrated this time and time again by allowing this guy to control her coming and going. If he was watching his son she had to pick him up at a certain time even if her son's father did not have to work and he watched him at her home. I asked her if she was crazy allowing this man to dictate how she lives her life.

She told me she did not want to anger him so things would run smooth. We started seeing each other and I told her something needs to change.

If he does not want to do right by you or your son tell him to get lost doing the majority of everything for your son anyway so what's the difference. She was in school working two jobs and holding it down I'm not sure if the dude was giving her child support and it was none of my business.

All I know you need to stop letting him take advantage of you. Dude already crushed her spirit by promising to marry her and reneged on his promise of marriage. This had a negative impact on our up and coming relationship.

She told me about some of the things he would say to her to crush her spirit and after a while it worked. Then she found out the dude was seeing another chick now who had two children. This guy was spending his time with this other woman and her kids buying her kids things and got her to ask her to marry him. The kicker was this woman was supposed to be one of his so-called friends.

Note to self and reader ladies not all men can be your friend and vice versa. It's crazy what women will put up with from men

She knew this woman and her son's father were friends but never accepted the fact he cheated

on her with his friend. This was evident in his treatment of her and his attitude towards her wellbeing. My girl found out about this and immediately went into I'm not good enough for anyone mode until we met of course.

It was difficult convincing her to talk to me let alone go out with me. Her birthday was coming up and I said to if you have nothing planned give me a call maybe we could go out. She called and experienced new life on our first date.

I could tell dude never took her anywhere we went to see Jamie Foxx perform live we loved it. Our problem was timing and trust she never invited me to her house and when we had time it was mainly spent at my house. Don't get me wrong the sex was incredible but sex is not something I ever lacked in my life every since I started having sex that's something I'm good at all the time. I'm not sure what happened but she started acting funny and we drifted apart. I ran into her at the bank with her baby daddy we spoke but not much.

She called me a week later with no number or blocked number she claimed her old phone in her baby daddy name was off and she was calling from her relative's house.

We spoke more and finally she got a new phone and gave me the number and we started seeing one another again briefly. It seemed we stayed in contact on the phone but made no concrete plans to meet. Through our dialogue I learned she fell back to the no one wants me mode. I asked if she was seeing someone else and she denied it. Finally she made it back to me I missed her and the sex.

We started seeing one another yet again but now she cut down a job and continued attending school which was great. When we met I wanted her to start school a while ago but she had no time. She would fit me in between leaving school and her days off at the job.

One day she let me know she was ready to have a child for me if she got pregnant. We were using condoms of course and as much as I'd like to have at least one child it would not be fair of me to get her pregnant and have her put school on hold.

Besides in the beginning of this book I stated I did not want to simply live with someone I want a wife before children. She is not ready for that type of commitment. Many women are willing to have children but don't want to get married. There is something wrong with that picture and that was my moment to bounce.

Note to self and reader Once two people fail to share the same basic relationship goals that would have no doubt affected one's future it's time to get real with one another quickly. I recognized where this was going and opted out before any decisions or mistakes were made.

We still talk from time to time but only superficially nothing deep. One never knows what the future holds. Besides she never admitted to her family she broke up with her child's father.

I found this very troubling simply put if you're still answering to your family and you're a grown woman with a child it's something wrong with that scenario.

BOUNCE 11

This brings me to another woman I met at a baseball game. My job took the employee for a day off. She had a headache from sun exposure when we met but none the less I still managed to hold her attention. It was a great day for baseball and apparently meeting women. We hit it off immediately after our initial meeting after she and her friends jumped in front me and my coworkers in line. After the game I walked her to the train we exchanged numbers and spoke on the phone for three hours and made plans to go on a date. After all we worked for the same company and she seemed sane at the time. I knew this was too good to be true and I found out why.

I learned she was married for a number of years and I was curious why there were no children. She explained to me she was unable to have children. I thought she said she may not be able to have children but once she explained things to me fully I understood completely.

I continued on with the relationship knowing full well this woman would not be able to bare any children from the jump that was my moment to bounce but I stayed perhaps out of loneliness or maybe I was tired of all the bullshit that crept into my life.

We had our first date in Manhattan and stayed out late. I was working two jobs and so was she when we started dating. It's interesting how we worked around the job thing initially and dated successfully. She would stay at my house during the week because it was easier for her to get to work from my house. It took two hours on the train from her home to arrive at work.

I would get home first and cook this seemed to become a pattern. I suggested if she was going to come over on a regular she needed to cook also. I met with a little opposition on that matter but she complied. On Sundays when she had to work she would go home on Saturday morning. I worked both weekend days so I really had no day off at all.

We worked it out anyway we could so we could spend quality time with one another. After all that's what people in like do for one another. We had not progressed to the point of love yet but we were getting there surely but slowly.

Once we declared our love for one another the sky was the limit, it was nothing she would not do for me and me for her at a moment's notice. I know you're asking what happened since I decided to stick around. Well once something is started it should not be changed up mid stream remember me saying that a few chapters ago.

We spent our first holiday together at her family's place. It was cool but was not a choice of mine and I could not see going to the same spot every occasion so I made it clear I'm not going out to her family's place for every holiday on a regular basis.

I have traditional plans I like to carry out every so often with my family. When it was time to share in my extended family holiday gatherings she did not want to attend and found every reason not to come with me. So the last time I asked her to come with me on a holiday she accepted. She met some of my friends that I consider family but she was so quiet no one knew she could talk. Normally she is not quiet at all I have to shut her up at times.

I know people are shy but sometimes it becomes very annoying when that person never breaks out of it around other people. It makes people feel like they are hiding something.

The final straw was she decided to test me and refused to come over my house until I came to visit her. She lost her job and started working at another job closer to her home but not as close to my house. Now it became a problem for her to sleep over my house or come and visit.

One day she showed up out of the blue late one night after she'd escorted some kids to an upstate prison to see their dad.

I knew then we were heading in two different directions. If it was ok for her to come to my house on that night why not come to my house like she did initially. My biggest problem is parking in her neighborhood. It was almost non-existent. I don't believe in giving the city my hard earned money through a ticket that I could have avoided in the first place.

BOUNCE 12

She admitted to me when she used her mom's car it took her hours to find parking five blocks away. When I took her home after our first date I had to use my now expired certificate to park so I would not get a ticket. When it was convenient for her to come to my house it was all gravy. The minute her job situation changed it became why you don't come out here sometimes. If it took you more than two hours to get to work from your home why in the devil would I want to repeat that commute she hated to travel daily.

Note to self and reader don't change things in the middle ladies and gentlemen. This confuses things and sends mixed messages.

She used this as her moment to bounce. We broke up when she refused to come to my home unless I came to see hers first. We had other problems that top the list that really were pressing but only discussed briefly by us. One day while we were in our bliss she asked me if I would consider adoption. I said no I have no problem with my plumbing, it's still intact. She on the other hand was less fortunate and I know that bothered her a great deal. I'm not saying I would never consider adoption but it would have to be the last resort.

I want the pleasure of participating in the action of creating a child and enjoying it because after that I'm told that's the last joy one has for about eighteen years or college whatever comes first. Although we were short lived in our experience I would not have traded it for the world.

I should have taken the opportunity to bounce when I found out she could not have children but like so many others I hung around probably waiting for her replacement. As I mentioned earlier I worked quite a bit often two jobs mainly to keep busy in between so called relationships. I became more immersed in the internet dating scene.

BOUNCE 13

I met another woman I came to be great friends with but the relationship was what I consider short lived. People reading this may think I never had a successful relationship. This woman had three teenage daughters all very nice except the youngest one. She was evil from the jump but polite nonetheless. We like the other women enjoyed one another's company and I traveled to see her whenever I could. Parking was never an issue when I visited her home. I guess that is a hang up of mine just as receiving New York City rip off parking tickets.

I think it makes the trip much easier and a smoother ride knowing one does not have to search for a space once one has arrived at their destination.

We did not go out much other than the movies or to the mall. She had a lot of health issues I found out about starting with a severe case of asthma. This stopped us from doing a lot but it did not stop everything. Like other women I dated with children they did not get in the way of us dating. In fact they were happy for their mom.

I like to think I brought balance to the household. I think at times she was a little restrictive and here I came offering my two cents. She listened and valued my opinion which I was happy to add. I was asked first I did not just offer it. She was very honest and secure in her own right but still had some hang ups about relationships and marriage.

She had been married once before and dated a bit which did not leave her scared but left her somewhat shaken.

I asked her if she wanted more children and she said yes except one problem: she had a hysterectomy after her last pregnancy due to complications and could no longer conceive naturally or any other way. I later learned it was the hysterectomy or her life literally

As time went on I noticed she had a lot of friends, male friends. I did not have a problem with her male friends being in my profession. A lot of my friends are female. It came to a point in our relationship that I felt sometimes she had too many friends. I hung out with her one time and she told me about a dude that was stalking her.

I was not crazy about that nor the guy that bought her drinks whenever she went to her favorite watering hole. I'm not one to turn down a freebee but sometimes one has to draw the line especially if you're in a relationship. We started to see less and less of one another after the talk about her being unable to have kids. She came to me and we had a serious conversation and you know what was next. She felt since she could not give me the child I wanted we should break up. I did not readily agree but had no choice. That was her chosen moment to bounce besides I kind of thought and felt someone was waiting in the wings for my departure. I have not had kids since that happened and she questioned me on it one day. My answer to her was I will not just have children with just anyone. Real talk some people should not be allowed to have children and some of the women I ran into after her and I was over were good candidates but we did not share some of the same basic principles I wanted in a mother to my child. Call me particular and I am but I've seen what happens when you're not particular. I've witnessed grown men crying over child support eating away their checks and they are still unable to visit or spend time with their child. I have managed to avoid that situation because of condoms, my friend's stories and friend of friends. The woman I did consider having at least one child with did not want any more kids because it was so tough raising them alone and I don't blame them one bit. I would have no doubt did what was required and more to raise my child but most women that already have children they raised the majority of the time alone do not want to go down the possibility of that road again. Again I can't blame them for feeling that way but the child loses also. Life choices are for everyone not just the privileged.

Note to Self and reader some people and its true are out for an easy payday coming from your wallet. I was always taught everything that looks good to you is not good for you. Some things are beyond our control but some things can be halted before they become an out of control issue.

BOUNCE 14

Another life choice I made early on was with a young lady I met while going to my afternoon job. We would see one another and finally I spoke to her I only had a few minutes before I had to change and punch in and get to work. We made time for one another before school. She lived in the outer boroughs and that was a long train ride for me. We would meet in Manhattan and hang out until her step father found out he objected to my very presence. I found that odd and not the regular objection but strongly objected. I guess he felt like any father would feel although she disliked him for no special reason which was normal. One day we decided to take our love to the next level. My cousin let me use his crib (my aunt's home) . We were both virgins and had no clue what to do. We took the train uptown to my aunt's home, which contained my cousins room found the key and went inside and proceeded to made ourselves comfortable. When I tell you it was comical trying to have sex with a virgin and you're a virgin it's a mess. We gave up I was unable to penetrate her not realizing some of the preparation that needs to go into getting a virgin ready for sex which I have mastered now. The day was not wasted. We returned to NYC and hung out and planned our next getaway that never happened. A summer passed and she changed into someone I did not know at all. That was my moment to bounce. Three years later I happened to come across her number I called her to say happy birthday and the same parents that did not care for me welcomed me with open arms. Apparently she became the girl from hell drugs included. They filled me in and expected her to show up for her birthday.

I was mild compared to the dude she'd gotten involved with after I bounced. It seems she was more ready for sex than I was and decided to steer her attention towards a rather larger in weight fellow Although we experimented we did not have condoms and surely would have been the parents of a child no doubt a grown up now. We reconnected for a short time and still had some sparks among us and yes we could not wait to get at one another three years taught me a lot. I grew up a lot and yes I used a condom and she had an I.U.D implant which I kept hitting hurt like hell. We caught up on the periods of our lives that we missed and started seeing one another again. Her parents were pleased as punch. It was the best thing since pockets and sliced bread.

Note to self and reader perception is everything her parents thought this dark skinned kid from the Bronx was trouble but little did they know trouble was in their own backyard alive and well. The same guy that she started seeing was the one that turned her on to drugs. Our summer romance was brief and I had no clue what drugs could do to you.

She disappeared from my life as luck would have it she ended up south of NY doing well. She was one of those people that needed to change their environment in order to stay away from drugs.

BOUNCE 15

This brings another young lady to mind. I have completely forgotten about our experience. I was introduced to her by a mutual friend that I worked with. She was a strikingly beautiful girl with two children at the time.

I'm not sure but when we met, it was a blind date I was shocked at how beautiful she was in person. We went back to my place. I made dinner and opened a bottle of white wine. We ate, drank, talked and laughed the entire time.

It was getting late but I was off for the next several days so I did not mind the lateness of the hour. We went through three bottles of wine that evening. I was not trying to get her twisted but she kept drinking. I told her to let me know when she was ready to leave. I mean it was really late. She started taking off her clothes and announced it was too late to go home and she preferred to stay if it were ok.

I pulled out the extra bed in the living room and gave her a tee shirt and shorts. I let her shower first returned to my room and went to shower after she exited and when I returned to my bed she was in it waiting for me. I asked her if she was sure she wanted to do this and she nodded and said yes. The next morning we showered and ate breakfast at the local diner. I asked her again if she needed to call her kids and what time did she want to head home? She said no she was alright and in no hurry this concerned me. I thought to myself day two this is a long ass date. We went to the movies and dinner talked more and I learned some interesting facts about her. In my observation she did not once try to contact anyone to let them know she was ok. We again returned back to my house after picking up several more bottles of wine. I started to get suspicious because I had experienced a previous girlfriend with a history of substance abuse. I started to recognize the signs of her alcoholic habits. My so called friend that introduced us called the second day into our date and cautioned me in a matter of fact way not to give her any alcohol. She claims she forgot to tell me her friend is an alcoholic and fresh out of rehab. My suspicions were confirmed at that point. I made it up in my mind not to place myself in that position ever again.

Did I leave you ask of course not I stayed during my moment to bounce. I sort of abandoned what I believed in at the moment to try and understand this woman. I did not want to kick her out in the street. So after I found out the other information I really did not know what to do. So I went with the flow but I did not buy anymore alcohol. I did not want to be responsible for her doing anything and blaming it on the alcohol so to speak.

I did not want to leave her in my home due to her addiction history. I also learned she smoked crack once upon a time. In my opinion once a person smokes crack it's difficult but not impossible to stop. The way she was acting she was about to go on a binge once again.

Once she finally let me take her to her mom's house the explosion started. She asked me to wait a second. I wondered why but soon learned her mom was screaming at the top of her lungs about how she's starting this crack and drug shit again. Before she could leave back out the door her mom shouted what about these kids they need you and you keep leaving them. She responded with aw ma come on I'll be back in a little while. Her mother said you said that three days ago and disappeared. I heard all of this as she headed to my car. She hopped in and asked me to drop her off.

I drove and she cried. I asked her what happened back there and she said my mother makes me so mad. She was unaware I have phenomenal hearing and I missed nothing. She had no idea that I'd been down this road already. In the short time we rode she opened up and I learned a lot more about her and some things I did not care to know. I'm not one to judge anyone on how they live their lives but anyone that leaves their children in search of alcohol, a date, or drugs, is not a good judge of character or has character during the time they are engaged in the use of illicit drug activity. I must say while we were together she was very supportive when my father died. She traveled south with me to the funeral. I think she used this time as a getaway period.

We arrived and my family instantly took to her. She helped my grandmother change a few diapers in the daycare. My cousin's were talking to her about hanging out but I put a stop to that quickly. I knew where that could lead and I did not want to explain to this girl's mother and children how their mother ended up in the morgue behind some random drug use.

One of my cousins ran home and got his girl and brought her over but she was not as fine as mine. I also bet his girl was not on crack either, just my luck right. I never witnessed her using but shortly after we returned I dropped her off home.

A few days later her mother called me to ask if she was with me. Her mom was pretty cool after we spoke and got to know one another a little. After I told her mom she was not with me she informed me she has not heard from her in several days since we returned. We talked for about an hour. I promised to help search for her. After we hung up I called my friend that introduced us and informed her of her missing friend. She told me of as few places she may be getting high. I'm not one to visit the local crack house but in this case I needed some reinforcement. I called my cousin to help me track her down not because he has skills but he too is a crack head. As the saying goes game recognize game in this case crack head recognize crack head hang outs I did not have to promise him anything I do not condone crack use or any illicit drugs. I did care about this girl and her mother was a cool person. I never found her but she surfaced from what I understand. She and I have not had contact in quite a while. When I did hear about her she got married to an abusive guy from what I understand and had another child. I simply refuse to have children with just anyone. I have not heard or spoke to her for a long time or the friend that introduced us. It was not hard to pick a moment to bounce where I should start. I was caught off guard to see such a fine ass girl waste her life getting high. I'm sure she has some underlying issue as to why she was drinking and drugging her life away. I did not get the opportunity to find out what sent her life into this downward spiral. If I were to pick a moment to bounce it should have been when I found out her history from the very beginning before my heart got involved.

Note to self and reader I am of the belief two people cannot co exist if they are into different things. A person using drugs will not remain in a relationship long with a non drug user. It is in all of us to try and remain in this kind of situation for support but after a while you learn this is not the same person you wanted a relationship initially. The changes will come you may not see them right away but little by little it happens

BOUNCE 16

This made me think about another woman I met some time ago only because we worked in a substance abuse center together. She was very nice and also had a teenage son. He was well spoken and very polite. She and I started dating and we had a nice time.

It was a summer evening and she wanted me and her son to meet and get to know one another. We hit it off real well. I would pick her up after work and we would head to my home again. I never visited her home. I found this odd after a while and one day decided to question that fact. Her answer to my question was never required. We spent plenty of nights and some evenings either out or at my home.

One day she surprised me with a gift that was for me but more for her. I must admit we got a lot of usage out of it but I never pictured her as the type. I asked her how she liked being a mom she said it was great but she would rather have had his father in the picture to help. I also found out his father was somewhat coming back into the picture. She reassured me without my asking there was nothing about he or she that hinted on re involvement with one another. I asked her how she felt about having another child. I think it was her initial reaction that really turned me off. She was almost offended at my request and suggested I find someone else for that job. I responded so it's ok with you that I get another woman pregnant. She said I would not have a problem with it. I was stunned to say the least but at least she was honest. That was my moment to bounce. I did not leave after that I wanted to see if I could sway her mind to my way of thinking. I started to think she only wanted me for sex and nothing further. We spoke and sometimes argued about the subject but she could not be swayed an inch. Finally I gave up and did not bring up the subject any further. I decided at the right moment I would end this but it really never came up. She was very agreeable and we always had a great time together. I had no clue how I would pull this off because I really did not want to hurt her but we did not share the same long term goals. I'm not the mean uncaring bastard some would make me out to be but in this case I did not see any other way out. We were at work one evening at my full time job.

She informed me one of her relatives was getting married out of town and wanted me to accompany her to the wedding.

This meant I would have to meet the family and that leads to future questions that I did not want to dodge or embarrass her or myself simply because I was unsure of our true status. This was my opportunity to end this and without hurting her feelings. The next day she asked me if I was going to purchase a new suit. I replied no because I would not be going with her to the wedding.

She said if it's the money I'll pay for your ticket. I became enraged at the accusation that I could not afford the trip. In retrospect I really could not afford it and was too embarrassed to tell her the truth.

We argued and she left my apartment very pissed off at my all of a sudden attitude. She called me a few days later and we apologized to one another but I still proclaimed I would pass on this trip.

She wanted to have dinner but I declined. I told her I needed time to think about where we're going. She was baffled of course but had no idea I was out of the relationship a long time ago. I bounced without bouncing if one can understand what I'm saying.

I now know it was unfair of me to use her in the manner I did. I should have been honest with her after we disagreed about having a child for me. We never really kept in touch after that, barely speaking at work and she resigned. I'm sure our relationship played a big part in her decision.

Note to self and reader I think most men prefer women that are up front and honest not to the point where she sounds aggravatingly disgusting like some guys are but can put her cards on the table without regret I know I do.

BOUNCE 17

This next young lady I encountered had a child and did want another child at this point in her life, which worked for me because I was not ready. It was something that I could not totally let go and trust this woman. I know it sounds crazy but on our initial meeting I liked her and she kept her word and called me out of the blue. I was really surprised to hear from her and had almost forgotten about her. We began our term as boyfriend and girlfriend which took a strange turn. One day I picked her up and we returned to my house. We were watching television and a couple of my boys showed up. I introduced them and we were all laughing and talking having a good time. The doorbell rang and I went down the stairs to answer it. This is where it gets crazy. A couple of days ago a girl called my house looking for a friend of mine she'd met and exchanged numbers. I let him stay in the room down stairs which did not last long but none the less I told him to stay until he got on his feet. The young lady called and asked for him and I was pissed because a lot of people were calling for the dude on my phone. I initially hung up angrily on her and she called right back saying please don't hang up. She introduced herself and told me the circumstance for which she was looking for him. Apparently he was the last one around her and her friend when her purse, he and another friend disappeared. She said she only wanted her identification back because it was hard to replace. She was in the army and needed her army I.D. I told her I would look in his room while she held on. I did not see her purse or any I.D. at all. She sounded very nice on the phone. She gave me her number and I promised to call her after I spoke with him. Truthfully I knew she would not get her I.D. returned to her at least not by him. She showed up out of the blue when my girlfriend was at my house. She took an instant liking to me as a friend so here I was stuck because my woman was up stairs in my room being entertained by my friends. I returned up the stairs and asked my brand new girlfriend if she wanted something to drink. She said yes so I went to the store and grabbed one of my boys. I explained the situation to him and asked him to keep her busy. I ran up and down the stairs making up excuses for most of the night why I did not invite her and her girlfriends inside.

She finally decided to leave when guess who walks up the street towards the house. My friend, the dude she suspected of stealing her purse. She asked him if he and his friend saw her purse and if so she just wanted the I.D. back. He replied with an attitude "I told Ray the other day when he asked me no I did not see or steal your purse". He told her when you and your friend got up and walked away me and my boy left. I knew that was a crock of shit because he came in with new things on and had no visible means of supporting himself. This is the same guy that tried to throw a girl out of my house in the middle of the night naked because she would not give him a blow job. So was stealing beneath him hell no. That night was finally over and my now ex girl had no clue what went on at all unless she read this and figured it out. We spoke a lot on the phone and I would visit her every time I had a chance. She was very scared of her child's father for some reason but she never told me why. I think he was a drug dealer but she never spoke much about him other than she wanted nothing to do with him. After a night of love making and breaking a condom she thought she was pregnant but it was a false alarm. She was not the regular I'm scared I'm pregnant it seemed more like the, if I am pregnant it may not be yours I just got that feeling I later confirmed my suspicions one evening I called her and she was not at work and it was not her day off. I would usually pick her up from work but lately our conversations were becoming far and few between. I called her to let her know I would pick her up and she declined the ride several days in a row. I really knew something was going on at this point. I drove to her job and waited until she came out. She was shocked to see me standing there and I was not surprised to see her walking with a guy towards me. I called out to her and she walked over and got in my car. The guy shortly walked over and asked her if she was ok before she could answer and I said if she wasn't he said I'm not talking to you. I knew he was a punk when he said that. As she asked him to wait in the car I rolled up the power window on her side luckily he complied. I did not have the even temper I have today. I would fight at the drop of a hat. I now know better with age comes wisdom and some lessons come with a price. She told me she did not want me to find out this way. I told her what I suspected and she could have come clean instead of playing these games. Unlike the other situations I did not feel bad about her bouncing in this case.

When we met she was not working and we spent a lot of time together but after she became employed it was a different story. I was once a final person meaning once we were over I would never go back. I have since changed my attitude and thinking. After she exited my car and some time passed I didn't miss her once she removed herself completely. I never saw nor heard from her again. I have not thought about her until this book I did not do anything to apologize for as for the girl showing up unexpectedly we became friends with no other attachments come to think of it I never heard too much from her again either after a few phone calls and lunch she insisted on paying for at all places Denny's. I think her unit was deployed and we lost contact. In any case I don't think either of those women were for me now or then.

Note to self and reader if it's too easy to walk away from a relationship even if one loves the other and is willing to work at it someone's heart is not in sync with the other one hundred percent.

BOUNCE 18

I'm of course not without guilt. I met another woman while working at one of my many jobs. We would flirt with one another back and forth. One night after work we decided to have a few drinks before I gave her a lift home. I had a beer or two and she ordered white wine. We talked about how we both hated the job but it paid the bills. We eventually talked about why each of us remained single. I told her I did not like to date people I worked with because it causes problems and she agreed and reached over to kiss me at the same time. I said what that was for and she said I was taking too long.

I viewed things between us as friends and had no intentions of dealing with this woman at least not on a personal level. I asked her where she lived and she said who said I'm going home tonight.

I knew where this was heading and I really wanted no parts of it without another stronger drink. I ordered another and proceeded to get my mack on. It didn't take much because she already had her mind made up and she wanted to fuck the hell out of me that night.

I should have stuck to my guns but as luck has it everything was going my way. I learned the hard way when things are too good to be true they usually are and boy it was way too good.

We did indeed do the nasty that night in every possible position I could imagine. I figured getting it while the getting was good.

Only one problem we used condoms except once that was my downfall. We started dating and I would after work either go to my house or out for a bite to eat. We were at City Island eating seafood when she told me she was pregnant with my child. I looked at her and said are you sure she said yes she was two months. I'm now a nurse by profession and know how to calculate the EDC quite well. I had no clue back then what an EDC was or how to arrive at it so I took her word for it.

Young men are so stupid and naïve here I was single owned my own home, car, and legally employed and stupid as hell a gold diggers delight. I had not figured out the game until a woman I dealt with that worked for the same company schooled me on the game this chick was running. The pregnant girl had no clue the other woman she called her friend knew me intimately and we came out of our relationship as friends.

We had a special bond and remained friends. She told me ole girl was four months pregnant but we were only dating for two months.

I told the pregnant women we were going to the doctor to find out how far along she was and if she was more than two months pregnant don't ever speak to me again. She demanded to know why I started asking about how many months she was really pregnant. She refused and said if you don't want to have anything to do with the baby that's your choice.

We shared a mutual moment to bounce and we never spoke again. She was eventually fired from the company and moved. I know in my heart of hearts that child was not mine and so did she. She saw a meal ticket and tried to latch on to me not knowing when people are treated right no matter if you're together or apart they will never turn their back on you. I thank god my ex girl told me the truth or I might have been one of those brothers that pay for a child for years only to find out the child was not yours DNA was not perfected yet. On anyone's behalf that's selfish to the child and the male that was captured in that trap. There was no question about me bouncing out of this woman's life as fast as I could.

Note to self and reader in my book any woman that would stoop so low to trap a decent man instead of holding the real father responsible gets no respect from me. I heard horror stories about guys getting trapped in these types of relationships not the bums that are once a year father on father's day but the good brothers that work and love their children only to find out the child's not theirs. I do not care what anyone says it's not the same once you find out it was all a lie to keep the money flowing. This cheats the child also and starts unnecessary questions sometimes when a parent is absent they need to stay gone.

BOUNCE 19

This invites another situation unlike the other experience this was drama filled from the beginning to the end. I met this woman once again while working. I worked in the field and she worked in the office. She was very inviting when we met and I accepted her invitation. I introduced myself and asked her if she would like to go out. She said she would have to see if her sister would baby sit.

We did not get to know one another that night but she called me and asked if my offer still stood a few days later. I was not doing anything or anyone so I said what the hell.

Over dinner I found out she heard some interesting things about me that were not true of course. It was up to me to set the record straight. I did not have a stable of women nor did I have a woman at the time. The girlfriend I did have turned out to be an undercover crack head and I sent her on her way after I realized it was a fight I could not win at this particular time. She told me her story which involved physical and emotional abuse from her children's fathers. She had four children and I had no problem with that but she did not readily want to tell them she was dating yet. I encouraged her to continue pursuing her GED and promised to help her with the work. She called me one evening and I was off and asked if she could come over to study. Of course I said yes.

She arrived and after a couple of compliments we got down to reading and studying. It got late and we both were tired but not too tired to handle our adult business.

The next morning a knock was at my door and it was a young lady that I had previously wanted to become monogamous with but she turned me down

She came bearing gifts but it was too late I told her I had company and we would talk later. She was civil and went about her business. We later spoke and she said she thought about my proposal and decided to give it a try. I had put off the young lady that spent the night long enough and she took too long. I told her if she would have only caught me yesterday it may have been a different story.

We spoke more but I was not swayed. She only wanted me because I was with someone else and the cat she was chasing told her to get lost. Understand she told me she was waiting for another brother she was semi involved with to come around.

Once that fell through she then wanted to cover the hurt with my company. I do not play second fiddle to anyone who never did and never will. One has to master the game to be a player.

I think because of her children, me and my new woman did not go out much, in fact I found myself at her home quite often under the premise of helping her study which was legitimate. I also tutored her children, the ones that were older. She made dinner and all of us sat at the table. She could not fry chicken for beans. I do not eat food that does not look appealing, taste good, or is bleeding especially chicken. When you purchase the large chicken legs they have to cook slowly on a medium flame. I also informed her large chicken legs were for baking not frying. I cooked dinner for her and the kids once and they loved it.

I'm an excellent cook. Don't get me wrong she could make a mean roast con pollo with beans and rice. We did manage to sneak out once in a blue but not much. One day I had an idea to have an outing with the cool people from work. We invited all the people we thought would show and have a good time no haters. I was collared by the job supervisor as the rings leader the next time I reported to work. They called me in the office to find out why I did not invite everyone from the job only to select people. Anyone reading this book that knows me understands why I said what I said next. My response was when all of you have your parties on the weekends and go out drinking after work not once was I invited but I heard about it the next day. The next time you have something, let me know and I will do the same and walk out. I was fired shortly after of course not exactly fired but all of a sudden my Virginia driver license was not good enough so until I got that fixed and obtained a New York license I could not return.

I still had my job at the hospital so I said screw them and never went back after that our relationship was still ok but now in the open as it should have always been.

It was difficult for me to watch guys flirt with her at work only because they did not know about us. It seems whenever I'm at a job and someone is interested in me it becomes a problem for those that were unable to get their flirt on.

Once I fled the spot it was on and popped I made sure all of them knew we were together. The studying came to a halt mainly because she got frustrated over the things she did not understand and would not put the extra effort into mastering the work. My visits became a little less and we were losing focus.

One night after a long busy evening at the hospital I decided to stay the night at her house. My friends worked at the same job I was "laid off from" so I waited until the coast was clear and headed to her house. I had showered at my friend's apartment downstairs so we went straight into her room. The next morning I waited until all the kids were out for school, got up dressed and headed to my mans apartment for a quick shower before I went home She was ready to head out for work and I was on the steps when her twelve year old daughter came screaming up the stairs like someone had hit her or something. I asked her if she was ok and she kept walking and crying. I continued to my friend's house and called my girl later to see what happened and she informed me her daughter apparently saw me and her mother in bed and became upset because she wanted her mother and father to get back together. The same father that was physically abusive to her mother. The child then ran to the grandmother and told her now the child's mother and grandmother were arguing about her involvement with me. I used most of the day to think about the situation and came to the conclusion this is my moment to bounce. I called her at lunch time and explained to her the best way I could. This situation can become very bad for me real fast because your daughter hints that I did something to her or touched her inappropriately and my life would be a living hell. I told her I was out, sorry I'm not willing to take that chance with an adolescent brat that wishes her father were still around to continue beating her mother like a drum whenever he felt the urge or became inebriated. She was upset but eventually understood besides the grandmother did not like the fact that my skin was black. The crazy thing was she was almost as dark as me isn't that a hoot. We parted ways and she came into my life years later asking for a favor. Apparently they moved and had come to visit but the people they visited did not have running water and asked if they could use my shower. I had no problem with it at all and once they finished she cleaned up. We talked and cleared the air after she showered and if I'm not mistaken she may have even apologized to me for not understanding why I broke it off with her at the time. I did see her at the hospital with a guy before that encounter or it may have been after it was her new man he was much older than she

She told me about him and how she found out he was an addict. I thought to myself your mother must have been proud.

Note to self and reader I think some parents are so twisted not to want their children to do better than they did. That includes education, relationships, jobs, child rearing, etc, etc. How could anyone not want their children to do better or live better? It would reflect the job one did raising the child into adulthood. It seems her mother was preoccupied with my skin color and race which caused so much friction in her daughter's home it was a pleasure for me to leave just so the women could have some piece in her life. In the meantime it's ok to have a caramel colored junkie in the house, how crazy and insane is that kind of thinking. She was catering to her narrow minded mother's way of thinking. If you like someone like them for them not their skin color. After our brief second encounter I never saw her again but I did see her daughter a few times around my neighborhood. She did not know I knew it was her but I recognized her with her new baby. If she only knew what she cheated her mother, brothers, and sister out of she would not have caused that rift between her family and this child was twelve years old at the time and was fully conscious of the problems she could have caused me.

Note to self and reader many people usually encounter this issue and I say weigh the facts and really be honest is it really worth ruining your reputation or your life to stay in a potentially harmful situation. I'm always careful when I get involved with a woman that has children. I look at how that woman conducts herself with the kids do they command her or does she have them under control. Any person with out of control children and the first thing out of the child's mouth and the last to me if I'm involved with their mom is "you're not my father." I immediately go into lock down mode and when they form their mouth to ask me for something and they will ask my response and it may sound cruel go ask your father. I feel like if a child is grown enough to try and be slick at the tongue and I'm helping to provide for them by all means ask your father for whatever you need. In my mind I'm thinking if he were worth anything he would be asking you if you need something.

I would not of course say that to a child but I'm thinking it. I'm not talking about a small child either. I've been lucky enough to never hear those words and I'm very good with children but if and when that happens oh lawd it's on. Please don't misunderstand me I would not treat a child mean or make them feel unwelcome but if a child lacks discipline and a certain level of respect for adults it's my job as a surrogate parent to provide guidance but before that happens a child has to understand you care about them and not trying to purchase their love and respect. My method is tried and true what about yours.

BOUNCE 20

I'm going to take you back to the first time my heart was broken and when I fell in love for the first time. I met this beautiful girl around the way I'd seen her with a knucklehead and I was not willing to wait to see if they were serious.

I got my friend's girl, incidentally her good friend, to introduce us. I always had a tight rap and if one could make a woman laugh you were in like flint. I did all those things and we were inseparable that summer. I worked and had money to spend on her for her birthday and just about anything she wanted. I never was a cheap person when it came to my girlfriend.

On her birthdays we spent together I took her on the spirit of New York cruise my friend and his women came along courtesy of me which he still owes me twenty bucks for their tickets.

I'm not one to beg for money that's owed you can never borrow money from me again and he never asked.

We did all kinds of things together I found out she started having sex early and got pregnant at fifteen.

Her parents talked her into having an abortion which she later regretted. We were like rabbits where sex was concerned it was no place she would not accommodate me and me her. This is how my sex life was formed anytime anywhere. I loved this girl and it felt great new love for the first time.

She called me one evening right after I'd walked her home which was strange I called her back to find out what was the problem. She wanted to see me right away so I hung up and headed toward her house. She met me halfway. I thought this must be serious. She burst into tears and I could not understand what the hell she was saying. It seems her parents decided to move south. I was devastated we both were in tears.

After the initial shock we devised a plan a stupid plan looking back but a plan. We knew if she got pregnant her parents and my grandmother would force us to get married which we planned to do anyway. We plan to put things in motion during the summer not thinking about the consequences. She also informed me her father told her if she got pregnant do not come back home.

When she arrived for the summer to visit her aunt I tried to get her pregnant. She told me her menstruation was late and she may be pregnant.

I had a friend that worked at Planned Parenthood. I called her and we went down together to get a pregnancy test and family planning if it were the case. When she came out of the office I thanked my friend and we left my girlfriend told me she was pregnant. Several days later I was at home when my friend from the Planned Parenthood center called to ask if my girlfriend had seen her period. I said I thought she was pregnant but my friend informed me my girlfriend was never told she pregnant. This is before all the confidentiality laws were put into effect and the truth would be told to all parties involved in the pregnancy.

This upset me because she lied to my face. She told me the test was inconclusive back then that meant nothing to me especially since she said she was pregnant. Once I found out the truth we decided she needed some self defense lessons because of the attention she generated and I would not always be around.

We went to the park. It was a nice warm summer day and I was showing her how to flip someone regardless of their size. After the demonstration she said she felt something and needed to go home because of a possible miscarriage.

I walked her home and my friend from the center called her aunt's home right after this happened. When I confronted her she said her period had come and she did not want to burst my bubble.

I of course bought the story but today I know it was nonsense. I don't understand why she did not trust me enough to tell the truth then we could have made it happen. I think that she may have changed her mind and that was the beginning of the end for us. We did not continue to try and get her pregnant after that I felt the trust was breached with that one lie. The end of the summer arrived and we vowed to stay together write, call, visit, all the things people in a long distance love relationship promise one another. In retrospect when I found out she lied to me that should have been my moment to bounce. I'd just started driving and bought my first car it was a piece of junk but it was my piece of junk. We would call each other and stay on the phone for hours we were still strong as far as I knew.

Soon as all long distance relationships do ours took the path of greater resistance the phone calls became fewer and fewer. As our paths encountered new people we expanded our base to include all who embraced us to fill the void. I happened to be home on this day she called and broke the news to me about a girl she mentioned many times as a good friend committed suicide.

It was a sad call. I tried to soothe her and it became apparent to me we as us were not going to get through this without physical contact. It's something about having someone to hold your hand through the tough times makes one feel more secure. My car would not have made it down south and her step father was less than crazy about me for some unknown reason. The next call I received after calling her for a week straight was her telling me we have to break up. My heart fell to my testicles and I was with the why. She told me she met someone and wanted to move on. I knew if I were not there to fill the void her friend took up in my absence it would come from some other place. I never thought it would be another dude we were supposed to be in love. That's not the first time I've been wrong. My moment to bounce was when she stopped calling and she was never around any longer when I called. I'm not stupid I knew dude was not fresh on the scene. The next call I received from her was telling me she's returning all my stuff to me wow what a way to cut ties. I received a box of things from her that I'd given her or she borrowed so she would not forget me. I guess she stopped looking in the box. Several months later she called and I was surprised to hear from her so soon. I just knew she was calling me to say she made a big mistake and she was on the way to NY. Nope I was wrong again it seems she was getting married and seen fit to invite me to the wedding. I respectfully declined of course and added I hope you're happy and I wish you much success in your marriage. I know she had moved on at this point but it was no sense in her gloating. Although she'd broken my heart I eventually moved on and it was very hard being she was my first true love. I eventually met another young woman and once again fell in love after some time. I was at home sleeping when the phone woke me and the voice made me sit up immediately. The voice asked do you know who this is I said no but the voice seemed very familiar. It was my first love calling me to reunite with baggage this time. We spoke cordially and she said she was coming to NY for a job seminar and asked if we could see one another. I said sure. I must admit I had some vengeful thoughts but I knew I would not be able to carry them out. We met and to my surprise this woman gained a lot of weight she fought to keep off. I'm not sure if it were baby weight or just depression from the picture she painted about her unhappy married life. She asked me how I felt about other people's children. I stopped her before she could go any further and informed her I'd moved on after she got married.

The look on her face was priceless I must admit. We ended the evening with me walking her back to her hotel room. I was a perfect gentleman and we never spoke again.

I knew it would have been a very big mistake for me to consider returning to this woman while she was trying to run away from her marriage.

Note to self and reader Time and time again people always return to where they are most comfortable. How many times have we ended a relationship and thought about the person we felt most comfortable before you realize your calling that person out the blue.. This applies to jobs or people we left behind, neighborhoods, non sexual relationships, and everything of comfort we know exist to us

BOUNCE 21

I had a friend that exercised the principle of returning to where she was most comfortable every chance she got. We met at a job I worked at and became friends only. I would often help her financially when she needed it. I admit I liked her beyond a mere friendship but nothing developed between us.

She was involved with a baby daddy but this guy was an abusive overbearing crack head. I don't know how many times she would call me to rescue her after he'd either tortured her or beat her.

One incident that stands out in my mind one day I was at her house it was around ten o'clock at night. He had just gotten out of jail and came straight to her house.

He walked in the living room where we had been doing some research on some law questions. I could tell he felt threatened by me because he commanded her to tell me it's time to leave and he also proved he was a chump.

I spoke directly to him and stated "why don't you tell me to leave". She looked at me and could tell I was ready to unleash every ass whipping she received from him that I picked up the pieces so many times. I remembered the last time I received a call from her she was at the hospital dude had been smoking crack and holding her and the kids hostage.

She claimed she was not smoking crack with him but no one can tell me a crack head and a non crack head can coexist.

She managed to get free after she threw her out the window she ran and called the cops. The kids were taken by the authorities of course while she was sent by ambulance to the hospital. The fall fractured her ribs and she also had minor scrapes and bruises.

She called me to pick her up from the hospital after being discharged. She smelled awful. She said he would not let her wash and it was evident.

After all of this and other times she stood between us and said Ray please go I looked at her in disbelief but knew this was a fight I would not win. I understood battered women syndrome but witnessing it up close was a beast. I said ok I'm out but I'll never darken your doorstep again. I never darkened her door again.

As I walked by him being the punk I knew him to be as I passed by he picked up one of his children and placed her between him and me like a shield. I wanted to crack him but like I said the fight was over before it got started. That night I bounced from this most unfriendly encounter and should have stayed gone.

About three years passed and I did not see nor hear from her until one day I went to buy pizza while on break from one of my many weekend jobs. I saw her and we spoke as if nothing happened. We exchanged numbers and she called me before the day was over.

We spoke in length about that night and it was not nice. After I'd gone he accused her of giving me a blow job. She said that night started another period of living hell with him. She again was physically abused by him and continued to take it. Finally she broke free after he displayed true crackhead fashion and stole all the kids Christmas gifts and her money leaving her high and dry during the holidays. This kind of friendship relationship is just as bad as a love relationship.

When she needed something I was the go to guy she would tell all her potential boyfriends friends about Ray and how we were great friends. She would tell these unsuspecting fools Ray will always come first before any other guy whether she was in a relationship with them or just friends. In essence I was the great friend she was the taker.

Needless to say our rather peculiar friendship ended with a strange phone call.

I was half asleep when she called and asked for monetary help. I responded with a few rather choice words. In short I was through with giving and continuing in this toxic friendship it's been at least five years since we've spoken. Sometimes it's better to end these kinds of things because after a while they become a drain.

In the long run looking back I was not helping her realize the damage she was doing to herself and our relationship by continuing to let her use me in that manner.

Note to self and reader Its nothing worse than helping a friend continuously that has nothing to give in return and I'm not talking sex either. When people know you have an affinity for them some use that until it either runs out or the other party gets smart enough to dissolve the relationship that was built on what can you do for me instead of can we help one another. I have a current female friend. We go out to have lunch, catch a movie and we respect one another's relationships if we are both involved with other people at the time. Has the question of a relationship ever crossed my mind about any of my female friends? I'd be a liar if I said no.

Note to self and reader One must remember once you have crossed that line from friend to lover it's almost impossible to return to only friends and most impractical. I've never been one to go long periods of time without having a woman not on purpose but it feels that way.

BOUNCE 22

I met this next woman at the Laundromat. It was a snowy winter day and we were practically the only ones in the place. My uncle was visiting from South Carolina and we found the only laundry open in the Bronx in the middle of a snow storm. I spoke to her and struck up a conversation. We finished our clothes almost at the same time even though she was there before me. I think she was hanging around for a ride because of the weather. The snow was pretty bad and I wanted to get home as quick as possible.

I told her goodbye with full intentions to give her and her two children a lift. She began to walk off when I jumped out the car and grabbed her cart, told her to get in and proceeded to drive her home. Once we arrived at her home I helped her with the clothes up the stairs a four flight walk up.

We exchanged numbers and I told her she would hear from me soon. I called her a couple days later and I ended up at her house after an early work shift. I liked this woman but her children needed discipline badly. We began going out and soon became a couple. She was unemployed when we met but managed to keep looking very fine. She finally received a job offer she'd been waiting on.

I took her shopping for some gear because what she was doing would be outside and as we know New York winters can be brutal. One day she came to my house and I was not home but she saw a car that was identical to mine.

She called and tried to end our relationship accusing me of cheating. I went to her house, picked her up and went back over to my house where the other car was still parked. Once she saw the other car had a roof rack the same color but I had no roof rack she apologized. We then made up and I loved every moment of it. We went out to eat a couple of times with the kids and it was a disaster.

The first time we went out with the kiddies she ordered their meals and we ate but her kids were picking at the food not eating. They wanted dessert and I said no dessert if you don't eat your food. The kids still did not eat she leaned over to me and whispered order them some desert after I just told them no to desert. I replied no I heard her say if I had my own money I would get it. I'm sure she was aware she said it loud enough for me to hear. Then she said maybe I should not have feed them. I asked her why did you feed them knowing we were going out to eat. I ordered them desert and told her the next time were going to eat don't feed them. The next time we went out it was to celebrate her getting a job. Those kids were acting the fool we saw two other children younger than hers sitting still talking quietly among themselves. I pointed this out to her and made it clear how her kids were misbehaving. She really did not pay me any attention and simply asked me to order them some desert. The kid's barely touched the food and this was not a cheap restaurant. I don't usually make a big deal over spending but I hate wasting money or pissing it away on someone's misbehaving children. Clearly this situation was not for me and I was quickly recognizing it my moment to bounce. I liked mom a lot but this was not going to work. It seemed every time I try to inject a little discipline in the boys she would coddle them and make it better. This should have been my moment to bounce.

Note to self and readers I've seen women make this mistake so many times with male children. They think by coddling them they are being nurturing but the problem is they do not know when to stop coddling. The boy is eventually going to become an adolescent with the same expectations that his mother is going to make everything alright. This child then grows up to be a teenager displaying the same selfish tendencies instilled in him by his mother and no father figure or a father that's over ruled by the mother to counteract the moms nurturing clear into adulthood. This is the same man women complain about there is no good men because mom never made him take out the trash, clean his room, wash the dishes, clean the yard, help the neighbor for free, wash the car, sweep, mop, wash his own clothes, and any other chore which allows him to build character and not become a lazy bum that looks for a women to be his MOMA. This is what this woman was setting up her sons to become if she did not correct her behavior as well as theirs. The last time she and I had contact she was dating a drug dealer once

I found out that I did not visit her again. I revisited in my mind why I bounced in the first place and never darken her doorstep again. None of the stories are in chronological order so if it seems like I'm returning to the scene of the crime I'm not. I've decided to tell these stories out of order because life happens out of order. I was a little reluctant to tell this next tale of woe but it kept nagging at me to the point I had no choice.

BOUNCE 23

It was a New Years Eve and my then girlfriend thought she was being funny by announcing at the last minute while in the middle of getting dressed to accompany me to a friend's New Years Eve party she changed her mind and "said I'm not going to the party." It was ten o'clock still early enough to make alternate plans but everyone making plans usually made them by ten. I left her house and called this girl I wanted to get with and had chased for a while but we both were involved with other people every time we tried to hook up. I knew things were over between my girlfriend and myself when she asked me if I was still going. I'll supply a little background on the girlfriend before I proceed. We met one night when I was out partying with a friend. I saw this girl dressed in white looking cute and me not being shy asked her to dance. We danced a few dances then talked a little. I told her I would offer to buy her a drink but she was still working on the one in her hand. I got her to laugh and smile. I knew I was in so far. We continued our conversation outside and ended up going to eat. I think it was some time ago. I drove her home and she handed me her number. I learned she had a child and for the most part was a single parent. I later learned the child's father lived in the same building three floors down. I do not like situations like that and I made it clear if she was still seeing dude we would be done. I know the mind set of some guys but did not consider she was still holding a torch for him. Their motto is once mine, always mine when children are involved. She assured me nothing of the kind would happen. I took her at her word until one day I called her and she was braiding his hair. When she called back I was furious and asked her why she was doing his hair. She did not see the problem in it which was a problem in itself. One day she called me and I told her I was at an ex girls home helping her wash her hair. She did not like it at all and proclaimed she would not braid his hair anymore. I really was at my cousin's house when this went down and she was washing her own hair. I really did not like lying to her but I had to put the mirror to her face so she could see the implications of her actions and it worked. After that I thought we got along famously until the New Year's Eve fiasco. She took the bus to my house and I would drive her home. I did not have much money to go out during those days but we kept ourselves interested watching movies or videos and talking. That worked for me but I like to go out and have fun especially if my funds were flowing. We talked a lot on the phone and I was glad to see her when she visited.

If memory serves me correct she lived with her mom and the child stayed between her home and the fathers house quite an arrangement right. The strange thing is we never argued or had a fight. I say strange because the way she started acting one would swear we were at odds with one another. That night she was acting very strangely. She never really gave me a reason why she changed her mind and I probed for an answer but never got one.

I finally left her house and called the other woman I mentioned earlier. She told me she waited for me to call but just made plans with friends. I went to the party alone and had a nice time. I called my soon to be ex to wish her a happy New Year she answered the phone and was still home.

Note to self and reader usually when someone is trying to create distance it's for a reason. It doesn't have to be a good reason but see it for what it's worth it's your moment to bounce. We spoke briefly and not too much longer after that the conversations became distant like she was preoccupied.

That was my moment to bounce and I jumped at the opportunity. I'm not sure what became of her but one thing is for sure she was very secretive that's not a real good feature in a relationship. I can't imagine dating someone with the same personality she displayed. When a woman cancels a date at the last possible minute with no better reason than I changed my mind especially after plans have been made and set in motion I'm glad it was not a wedding.

BOUNCE 24

This led me to the woman I called and tried to persuade her to join me at my friends party. We got together dated for a little while but her schedule and child really did not permit her much time for any extracurricular activities. We spoke when she could and dated on and off whenever she was available. I later found out she was still carrying a torch for her child's father once this became clear to me my moment to bounce became very clear. Another situation I became acquainted with was a young lady that had a child and we also worked on the same job.

I really had no intentions of becoming involved with her but as situations go we were thrust together. I remember it was at an outing we connected after I dislocated my shoulder. She drove me home insisting I go to the emergency room.

The shoulder was an old injury that I'd dealt with not long ago. I thought I knew what to do. It turned out It didn't work. She checked on me the next day by then I'd driven myself to the hospital.

The next time I saw her she made it clear to me she and her man were no longer together. I assure you I had nothing to do with them breaking up. We started talking and soon dating. Soon she started working at the hospital where I worked. I don't recall us going out much but we spent a lot of downtime at my place. It became clear to me quite quickly she had very strong feelings for me. I was not afraid but the fact that someone could feel so strongly that quickly made me back up a little.

As outspoken as I was I'd also faced heartbreak in my life and like everyone else I became gun shy. I never expressed my true feelings to her and when she told me how she felt I did the opposite and acted like an idiot. Although she had a child from a previous relationship her child was never around during our courtship and never became a factor.

I never doubted her feelings for me but I doubted my feelings for her. She sent a friend to find out how I truly was feeling about her. This was a mistake.

I knew these words were going to get back to her but I said them anyway. The conversation went as such. How do you feel about my friend? I responded I don't feel the same way she feels is what the friend heard. I'm sure after it was repeated it did not get back to her the same way it was said. What she forgot to add was I like her but I don't love her at this point in our relationship.

I used that as my moment to bounce because just as I'd predicted she started acting funny instead of coming to me to discuss whatever was bothering her. She started seeing this married guy on the job confronted by the wife and everything.

If she had come to me from the beginning and talked to me instead of sending her friend to find out what I was thinking and how I was feeling we may have salvaged a decent relationship. I admit it was a bitch move on my behalf and I offer no excuse.

Note to self and reader often people beat around the bush or include others in their relationship instead of talking directly to the person in the relationship. Communication always works when people are willing to explore that road to reconciliation.

I have heard more stories that consistently involve people not listening to one another.

It is of the belief of some people if two people do not argue they do not care for one another. It's that mindset that leads people to yell and scream at one another and nothing gets resolved.

BOUNCE 25

Take for example this young lady I came to know quite intimately.

She would always want to argue and fight about something if I said left she said right. We met at a club and I brought her a drink and we danced. She gave me her number sometime that night and we began to talk. Soon like any other union we became closer to one another.

I would pick her up from work sometimes when I was off. One day I arrived early to see her sitting and talking to some guy who remains nameless to this day. I witnessed her get out of his vehicle and stand where I usually picked her up after work. This time I was across the street because there were no spots available, remember I was early. I drove around the corner and picked her up where she always stood. We usually kissed when she got into the car but this time I skipped it and she said nothing.

After that I noticed every little thing caused a conflict. I asked her what the problem was and she said nothing. I asked her again why all the drama and she again replied what are you talking about. This was two-three days after I saw her get out of this car.

I got tired of the cat and mouse and finally said to her if you're trying to start a fight to leave let me save you the trouble. This was my moment to bounce. I don't know who the guy is you're seeing but if he wants you tell him to come get you. That's when the real fireworks started. She became upset because I accused her of seeing someone.

I sat calmly until she finished her posturing and moved in for the kill. I was skillful in my approach. I said to her I bet you didn't know I arrived early the other night I picked you up from work. The look on her face was priceless with that she said I could explain.

I'm not one for explanations I told her I did not want to hear it but if it's any consolation I hope you two are very happy. I still maintained my own residence although we spent most of our time at her home she had cable and I did not at the time.

I stood up and she said don't you want to hear my side. I said no because if you had any integrity or respect for our relationship you would not have gotten in another mans car for any reason and you would have told me before I told you.. As I walked away exercising my option to bounce she had tears in her eyes apologizing to my back. It was hard to walk out of there but for my own sanity I had to leave the situation. I'd been through too much bull to stay or listen to anymore lies.

Note to self and reader if one shows no respect for their relationship or the other person the relationship will never work. Understanding this action sets them and their mate up for a sudden crash in their relationship. When we do not exercise restraint correctly towards another male or female while in a current union the results are almost always disastrous. The person is asking to get caught in a position which leaves no recourse for real brothers or sister not to put up with the bull and exercise that moment to bounce.

BOUNCE 26

This next situation is up for discussion, maybe even a debate. I met this woman with several children. I've never been afraid of women with children but this chance meeting was right but went all wrong.

I don't pretend to know all the answers to raising children but I recognize when a child should be seen and not heard. It's clear children need boundaries and not friendship from their parents. I don't care what anyone else does but I'm not trying to be friends with a child I'm parenting. The children's mother and I got along well except when it came to the children. We disagreed a lot is an understatement. How can one tell a child one thing then almost in the same breath you're letting the child do exactly what you told them they couldn't do a minute ago?

This is the problem I had with this woman. When I tried to intervene she would try and overrule what I said by saying I told him it was ok. This was getting tired real fast and so were we. Now I understand the man that goes out for ice cream and never returns living under similar conditions. Instead of killing someone he just starts over somewhere else where he gets some respect. I'm not saying it's right but I understand his actions. As I said earlier I always kept my own place just in case. I've had friends come to my house to stay the night after they were kicked out by their significant others. In order to keep the peace they just left before the police arrived. It got to the point when it came to the children I discovered she made secret decisions.

One day the shit hit the fan when I told one of the boys to clean up the kitchen and he replied my mother said I don't have to listen to you. He was not supposed to let me in on that bit of information but low and behold the cat was out of the bag. My first response was to slap the taste out his mouth for being a smart ass about it but I realized this came from his trifling mother not the child.

I did what any other responsible person in that situation would do. I packed my rags I had at her house and took my black no children having ass home and did absolutely nothing.

The next twenty-four to forty-eight hours I said nothing to her, no call, no correspondence between us whatsoever. She finally came to my house one day after work. I did not let her in because I did not want her to think we had a chance. Finally she met me at work in the parking lot and asked me what was wrong. I walked past her and got into my car. This really pissed her off. She then tried to embarrass me. She soon found out that was not possible. I have a thick skin. She sent one of her friends to try and talk to me. I finally broke my silence and told her friend all the things that went on between us that prevented us from growing together as I would build she would tear down. The friend had no idea her girlfriend was so selfish but also shared a bombshell with me. This information of course changed the game for the moment. When we finished talking I gave the friend my demands if her girl wanted to talk to me. I guess you're wondering why I did not bounce. Her friend told me her girl was pregnant and I wanted to resolve this and make a go of the relationship for the potential unborn child. It turned out she had a miscarriage at least that's what she told me I think she was a liar. Things between us had not really improved and when I resumed coming over she simply sent the kids to their rooms or outside. Once I was sure she was not pregnant, that's when I bounced. We never spoke much after that and she has had problems with her kids back and forth in court, she is now a grandmother. I ran into her at the supermarket and she gave me her new number. I hold no ill feelings towards her but I simply do not date grandmothers young or old, hell my grandmother was still alive at the time. I made that clear to her during one of our few conversations while she caught me up on events that shaped her children's lives.

Note to self and reader when people want to confess their shortcoming shut up and listen; you may get an apology out of it. She admitted the mistakes she made not allowing her sons to take responsibility for their own actions or allowing any positive male role models she encountered through her life to influence her kids. She admitted by taking up for them right or wrong, not allowing them to face consequences and allowing them to do practically anything they want turned them into irresponsible men. Now she was raising her grandchildren and still allowing her kids to depend on her. I don't know about you but I could not wait to move out on my own when I was a teenager. I would see her now and then but we have not had any phone contact in several years.

BOUNCE 27

I met this next lady through a friend and his wife. I saw a picture of her and liked what I saw and wanted to meet her. We were invited to a mutual gathering and hit it right off.

I did not mind the travel to and from her home. We eventually would spend weekends together and planned to take trips. We would do the regular couple thing with conversations about child rearing. One day we were discussing having kids together and somehow we got on the subject of babysitting. I said it's not babysitting if it's your own child. She then said something that shocked the shit out of me. She said her mother would leave her with the babysitter or neighbor and her father never watched her when her mother went to work or went out. Then made it clear to me if we had a daughter she would not allow me to watch the child if she was to go out or to work. I found that very odd for someone to say let alone admit something so strange. The more I thought about it the more offended I became. I later brought up the subject again because it troubled the hell out of me. I decided to probe this a little more. I asked her if her mom suspected her father of doing something unsavory when she was young. She said no I again asked if she ever asked her mother was it something about her father she was not told.

She of course was offended but I did not care because we were now in a heated discussion on this subject. The discussion turned into an argument that night. After I learned of this not so minor detail we started to see and talk to one another less and less. She borrowed a video from me that was never returned after we kind of fizzled out. She used that moment to bounce that one little detail or dare I say character flaw on my or her behalf made a big difference to the both of us depending on whom you talk to about how things went down. This is not to say all of my relationships were sexual. I've dated a lot and noticed early on something was not quite right with this individual.

Note to self and reader once certain information is discovered about serious life decisions do not pussy foot around. Either you agree or disagree with one another and if it's something that will affect the children down the line a decision must be made. Please be clear and honest with your significant other and if it cannot be resolved it's time for one of you to bounce.

BOUNCE 28

One woman I met loved to go out and eat wash clothes at my house for free and be treated like a queen under the pretense of us dating. She failed to realize one thing that was not going to last forever especially since we were not an exclusive couple either you like the one you're with or you don't.

One cannot have it both ways although many people like to think they can. This woman would after a while call me like we were engaged to one another. She was very vain but at first she was very nice and smart about her game. I discovered she was lazy and wanted others to take care of her as if she were dipped in gold. I have no problem taking care of anyone but they have to take care of me too if you know what I mean. We were never intimate but she tried to dangle the hint of sex so I would stay around. I started to ignore her calls and finally they stopped, never laid eyes on her again and did not wish to unless she had grown up.

I suspect she thought she had me on the hook while she dated someone else that treated her like garbage but she still held on to him. Remember I told you we were not exclusive to one another. Once her nonsense became clear to me, that was the moment to bounce and I did without regret.

Note to self and reader I will never understand for the life of me and I'm sure millions of other men will agree. Why do women stay with the guy that treats them like shit? I guess some women have been conditioned or conditioned themselves along with their low self esteem to just take it. When a guy comes along and treats them like a lady they do not know how to respond. I've actually had women tell me I'm too good for them. I did not understand that statement for a while until I discussed the subject with a friend of mine. I have never thought of myself as being too good for anyone or vice versa.

BOUNCE 29

Another woman I met in passing would have been a great fit but she displayed questionable behavior while we were out eating. She tried to order everything on the menu like she had not eaten in days maybe she didn't but we were on a first date and last date she just didn't know it yet.

The conversation was minimal but the eating was plentiful. As I said earlier I'm in no way a cheap guy but damn the first date is usually reserved to put your best foot forward.

During dinner it became clear that she had indeed put her best foot forward and her mouth followed. She was not remotely interested in the bill or how much it cost. She definitely made sure to order enough so food would be left over to take home.

This woman had the nerve to tell me she had a great time. She wanted to know when and if we are going out on our next date. I honestly had no answer for her only I'll call you

Note to self and reader If we were getting to know one another on our first date ordering a lot of food for which I was grateful she ate most of it is a big turn off. That was my moment and I of course took it like so many others if I'd ignored this one I most certainly could not and I felt justified in my action.

BOUNCE 30

Another woman I ran into from back in the day we never dated until that chance meeting. She was great but she did not like New York and was running every chance she got to get away. We went out and started spending a lot of time together. We were not boyfriend and girlfriend but we were getting there fast. She then decided to leave town with her job and finish raising her daughter. She raised a wonderful respectful polite child now on her way to graduating college.

I was not ready to pick up and follow her so she moved on to another situation which worked out very well for her and her daughter. She knew it was her moment to bounce when I would not go with her and I respect her for making that move. I guess in hindsight I made the choice easy for her to make.

We remain friends to this day and I would never impede on her new marriage. I however took the marriage road once and have not decided to run that race again just yet.

I know some may wonder why I have not used fictitious names for this revealing book because I believe changing the names would change the identity. Those I refer to are real people and once they read the stories and if they remember any part of our failed collaboration they will know whom I'm talking about. Everyone searches for happiness in their own way and if they are lucky achieve a glance at it while some seem to attain it as easily as taking a breath.

BOUNCE 31

This next friend of mine like so many others chased happiness and if I left it up to her we would be happy according to her definition of happiness. We met on a job I was assigned to after leaving my hospital job of many years. She was in the medical profession but not a nurse. We did not spend the customary time dating or eating out. We were not over one another house constantly. She made it very clear she only wanted sex but the catch was it was not only when she wanted it but I could call her and say I'm on my way and she would have no problem with it. I know most men would have jumped at this opportunity and I did but I found out the relationship was one sided. I like going out and doing things and she found it hard to leave the house anytime I suggested we go do something. She really never had to leave the house. She had food and everything else delivered and worked out of her home. I quickly realized she had a problem. At first I thought it was about us being out then it hit me like a ton of bricks. This woman is a partial recluse on her way to full time recluse. I learned that she requested to work from home full time and her job was considering it because she already worked four days a week from home. Once I learned this information I tried everything in my power to convince this woman to go out and do things but she would not budge. One day I did not show up when she called nor return her calls. I finally called her a few days later. I told her I was sick and unable to move until today. This heffer replied when you better come see me and hang up the phone. If I were really sick and depended on her I would have been in trouble. I'm sure the readers have figured it out by now I had to bounce from this poisonous relationship had I stayed and accepted her terms.I would have become her reclusive partner. The thing this woman failed to realize sex and love are two different things. She fed my sexual side while my adventurous side remained empty. She made good money and offered to pay for my further education if I considered moving in with her. She said all I had to do was attend school and of course sex ercise on demand and she would do everything else. I know that sounds like the perfect picture but I was not raised to sponge off women as crazy as this may sound. I get a good feeling when I look at my bank account because I know I earned every cent honestly. I also know when someone offers something like that a string is always attached.

Note to self and reader ladies and men reading this book please understand no one gets something for nothing. I've seen guys fall into that trap of letting their significant other take care of them. It is not pretty when that person does not hear what they want. I'm not trying to get preachy or anything but I cannot say it no better than the words I write. I wish someone would have written a step by step manual on how to avoid love pitfalls but the truth is no one can be that clever. I don't care how many male to female relationships one experiences, everyone is different. The key is to learn from these encounters and not repeat love mistakes.

BOUNCE 32

My next love mistake was thinking I could accept someone for themselves and change them if need be later on if we survived. I met this woman while out with a friend. I ended up meeting another woman. We were at a dinner and the woman sat right across from me. She was very pretty. I have a weakness from pretty women. While everyone got up to dance we started a conversation and discovered a lot about one another. A song came on and she asked if I wanted to dance. I noticed she was tossing back drinks and was still quite lucid. We both got up and I noticed she was walking kind of off balance and danced off balance.

I had a few myself but not enough to be considered drunk. After we danced several dances and exchanged several numbers we made plans to date. We spoke back and forth on the phone for a couple of days and it was nice. I arrived at her house finally for our date. I was in for the shock of my life when she came to the door she had the same walk but this time she had a brace on her back then it hit me. She was handicapped. I honestly do not know how I felt at that revelation that very moment. All I know is I never imagined dating a handicap girl in my entire life. That means the night I met her she was not tipsy she was dancing the best of her ability. I also met her son that night, a cute kid. When I called my best friend and told him about my date with a handicap woman he laughed until he cried although it was a good date, one of the best I'd had in a long time. I truly do not discriminate but the funny part was I did not realize she was handicap until the next time I saw her. After our initial date we spoke on the phone a lot but I was busy with school and found it increasingly harder to find time to spend with her and we eventually stopped talking. I did not bounce. I was really focused on my studies. I later ran into her when I was giving flu shots at a place where she worked. I of course made excuses as to why I found it difficult to call her or make time to call her. She gave me her number again. I did not call her and had no intentions of calling her. I know it sounds cruel but I still could not see myself dating a handicap woman then it hit me. I've always dated handicap women. It's just that hers was on the outside and there was mental or it could have been me.

Note to self and reader all of us are handicap to a degree when it comes to relationships. We move as far as our experiences led us then we are flying solo that's when things go astray. Since love or feelings do not fit neatly in a box for us to take out and put back to fit all occasions we end up all too often not seeing it through and letting it go.

That is different from recognizing when someone is not good for you and leaving an unchanging situation. People often use that as a means to bounce but under further examination of themselves and the other person it's something much deeper happening. I was fortunate to recognize my bullshit and theirs too. So when it's time and the other party says wait my response is wait broke the bridge.

BOUNCE 33

My next steps to foundation building came at a party when I was introduced to a woman my friend thought I would like. I'm not sure what type of women my friends think I like but this clearly was not my kind. I like independent women but this woman would not shut up about how she did not need a man. So being the blunt individual I am I asked her how do you please yourself. I know I caught her off guard but I was tired of her male bashing at will. She of course called me a child and refused to answer me but I could not resist and answered for her. I accused her of using her middle finger because that's the only thing that could stand to be around her. She flipped out and became verbally abusive. I called her out in front of all our friends and she was unprepared. A few weeks later my friend told me that a young lady wanted my number to apologize to me. I told my friend to tell her no harm no foul I knew we would have eventually dated but I wanted no parts of her at all. I pre examined the situation and for all it was worth, I did not see any good coming from it because she was damaged goods and until she got some help she would be no good to anyone. My opinion is women that yell I don't need a man are lying to themselves. They don't need the man that put them through the rough time they faced I agree. That's the baggage women can't seem to separate when it comes to men and relationships. This particular woman accomplished a lot educationally but those degrees can't make her feel like someone asking her how was work or rubbing, feet and shoulders. I don't need to go further. Until she either seeks help or recondition her thinking she will not achieve any success in the dating arena. Another aspect she hit on was oral sex and how if a man wanted someone to suck his dick he should ask his mother to do so. I was truly offended I love oral sex and I took great offense to that remark and that's why I cut into her nonsense.

Note to self and reader I'm not saying people have to agree with me but something like that is intimate between people that love one another not just anyone you chose to share your bed with for a quick one. When I hear that nonsense I know that person has not truly experienced true love, only superficial feelings making it difficult for them to fully give themselves to another.

She was bitter and hurt a deadly combination and a recipe for relationship mayhem. The flip side of that is something traumatic happening involving oral sex for which they may not ever get over. In that particular case they may not ever experience a healthy relationship because they are still damaged goods. I have nothing to lose by calling it what it is in plain terms.

I've made it a point in life to never go back into an old relationship but have since changed my attitude which I said in an earlier chapter. It's not because of any phobias or unlucky beliefs. Once I believed like many others I usually put my all into it initially then what else can I give the second time around.

Note to self and reader I've come to learn certain people have the ability to change and it may be worth reconnecting with them to see if they have abandoned some of those ways that have stopped them from having a successful relationship myself included.

BOUNCE 34

This made me remember another woman I dated briefly all because of my birthday. It was October and my birthday I had tentative plans with my woman to go to her house after I was finished at the barber shop. The exact words she said were: ``If you're not busy after you finish, stop by my house. While I was in the barber chair I began to feel uncomfortable. It seems I ate some bad chili and my stomach began to rumble as a result diarrhea soon followed. Instead of going to my woman's house as planned I proceed home to shower and make myself feel fresh and clean. I did not call my women because our plans were not concrete. She asked me to stop by but due to the circumstances I returned home. I went home, did my thing and probably went to sleep while watching television.

The next day I reported to work and received a phone call from my women cursing me out for not coming to her home. I mean I was every son of a bitch, MF, asshole, dumb ass, etc; I of course hanged up and used my moment to bounce at that point. She and I are cool today but she did not give me a chance to explain why I did not come to her house until I ran into her months later. I had no idea she planned a party for me. She also told a mutual friend the gift she bought me was a Sean John suit and returned it after I did not show up. I explained to her I've never in my life had a birthday party that I can remember and on top of that diarrhea is no joke I felt terrible that day. I admit I dropped the ball when it came to calling and informing her I was not feeling well. That fact she flipped out over that nonsense I was glad to go I refused to have someone curse at me for silliness and then apologize like that is supposed to make everything alright. I'm so tired of these records that allow people to apologize for the horrible thing they did or said to someone then apologize it away. When the opportunity for us to try again came around I passed right away.

Note to self and reader people must realize when to never re-enter a relationship problems that were unresolved are destined to repeat themselves. People rarely change as they get older especially if they never realized a problem existed. I'm in no way saying people cannot change but it's very difficult. These things need to be revisited by both parties before a relationship level is reached.

BOUNCE 35

I recently spoke with someone that was forced to bounce from their relationship. I guess I should give you some background information on this relationship and how during this courtship from the beginning in my opinion there were several times this brother could have and most certainly should have escaped this union. The readers of course can judge for themselves. I received a phone call from him and we started with the usual pleasantries then he laid it on me about what went down between him and the woman he was about to embark on a life journey or as he put it the next phase of his life. He had not been out of a relationship long before he and she started talking and from what I was told they spent hours on the phone. If you had not guessed yet it was a long distance relationship or what I like to call union killers. They had met once during a trip and they were both in relationships but managed to reconnect with one another after they were free. I'm not sure how that worked but it worked for them. They had been talking for a while and had one visit with one another. You know, a romantic weekend. Well it seems he missed a call with her and went out with a business partner for a meeting. They had dinner and were given free passes to an event. When he returned he phoned her and told her about the event and why he failed to answer her call during the show. This woman went off, she accused him of being a homosexual with his business partner among other things. I will not repeat the things this woman blurted out of her mouth. I don't know about you but that is a deal breaker but no my man stayed and pleaded his case. That was his moment to bounce but he decided to stay and work it out because he loved this woman. After a series of arguments and disagreements one day they were out and of course discussing their future together. Over the weekend some events transpired that were petty in nature and she felt he did not have her back. He has since moved and they live closer to one another. The conversation got heated at one point as they were walking towards her car. She put his bag on the ground without saying a word and drove off. She decided that was her moment to bounce. I'm not sure what precipitated her course of action and I probably never will but to leave someone stranded in the street.

My question is how does one go from being in love with a person one moment and not care enough to make sure that person is ok the next? Ladies imagine if your girlfriend called you and said she was left on the curb after a disagreement with her boyfriend.

I don't think you or anyone else would have a kind word to say about him. This could have been avoided if he'd only bounced when he was accused of being a homosexual earlier in the story. Love makes one do strange things and in this situation very inconceivable things.

Note to self and reader sometimes when an out is given its best to take the out and chalk it up to another love experience. Do not force a love connection it will not fit.

BOUNCE 36

Another one of my first loves was a girl I met through a friend I was giving advice to try and get her. I was finished with another tiring trifling girl when she fell in my lap so to speak. I kept hearing him go on about how fine she was and how she would not give him the time of day. I went with him to check out this girl and damn she was fine, smart, and liked to laugh. She had local dudes sniffing around and her mom did not have a problem with boys hanging around her house after her daughter to which none had a chance. Our introduction was an anger filled moment. It seems her family was at war with the family down stairs and as me and my friend were walking up her mom came outside with a pitch fork. I deemed her mother pitchfork Annie after I witnessed her in action. I still was not afraid of her mom but kept my guard up. Once I cleared out all the suckers my friend included she and I started dating. We had a great relationship but mom was against it from the start. We tried to spend a lot of time together but met resistance. Her mother all of a sudden did not want me in her home. When I visited I now sat on the stoop and my girl came outside but to my surprise one day her mom came down stairs and cursed me out in front of the entire neighborhood. Out of respect for her mother I said nothing in return and went home. My girl called me and apologized and of course all was forgiven. We then started leaving the block and taking walks. I still had my piece of car and we took rides sometimes. I found out later that her mother was jealous of our relationships because I bought her daughter things and took her out when her mother allowed it. The old dude her mother dated did nothing for her, did not even take her to a movie once in a while. We had to start becoming cleaver in our sneaking around. Then my uncle David gave me some advice he said bring her mother a gift and watch her attitude change. I'll be damned I was the best thing since cuffs. I later found out her mother was making my girl's life a living hell as long as she and I were dating. I was young and hard headed but in retrospect I should have bounced and let her live in peace. We managed to hang in there and I eventually met her father during her graduation from high school. Dude was cool, he understood his daughter was fine and going to attract somebody and after he and I met he was glad I was not a knucklehead.

She went off to college and when she would come home all of a sudden her moms would get into a cleaning frenzy. She got tired of it and moved in with me between semesters her mom stopped speaking to her for a while. We went through our ups and downs nothing serious but she decided to quit school. We agreed initially she would attend school first then I would attend college. We did not make it to that point we eventually broke up but remained friends. The crazy thing was years later her mom started asking about me like I was her best friend. We tried to get back together one winter in the Bahamas but it did not work out. We had an argument which was rare for us.

We decided to go snorkeling and scuba diving. I was taking off my clothes and she was reading. I asked her if she was going in and she said no she could not swim.

I offered to teach her to swim. I told her the life jacket would keep her up and I would be in the water with her but she still said no. I went in and left her a barracuda came too close to me and I got out the water to see her putting on scuba gear.

I asked her why are you putting on scuba gear. She said I'm going in and the captain is going to show me how to swim. I flipped out and said you're willing to trust a total stranger who was clearly out of shape to teach you to swim rather than someone you've been with for years.

After that conversation she decided not to go in the water. The captain apologized for causing the conflict between us.

Note to self and reader sometimes a good idea should stay just that idea. This was one of the incidents that formed my leave the old behind not to be revisited but I did not take into account some do grow wiser with time. She years later apologized to me finally understanding my point of view. We both shared moments to bounce but we were young in love and head strong the curse of a Scorpio man and woman.

BOUNCE 37

I almost forgot about this woman I met over the internet. We talked on the phone for a while then one day she was gone. I thought okay this is my moment I mean it was two weeks and no return calls. Then one day she called and I was at work. I was surprised and delighted. I thought I may have pressured her too hard to meet but I later found out she was broadsided by a truck and was in a coma for a week. She suffered multiple injuries and was unable to walk under her own power. I offered to help her out several times but she declined. When she was up and around I suggested we meet this was about eight months into the relationship she proclaimed her love for me and I returned the saying. I really don't believe one can fall in love over the phone sight unseen. She kept coming up with all these excuses for not wanting to meet. I finally got tired and during one of our conversations I told her to shit or get off the pot. I was not so interested in the sex but I like to look into the eyes of the person I was talking to at least once. I learned from the past that long distance relationships do not work. She again declined my invitation and I was forced to tell her I was ready to bounce. She was hurt but I needed something tangible. We have not spoken until recently when she called me to find out whose number she was dialing. I promptly introduced myself and we carried on a conversation about one another's lives like we never stopped talking. It seems she'd moved on and was happy as I. She explained to me she was scared and was not ready to start anything new at that point. I asked her why did she dangle herself in front of me like a carrot instead of being upfront and honest from the start. She apologized and asked if we could have lunch in the near future when she comes to NY. I declined and she could not understand why. I told her our moment has passed and it really makes no sense to revisit something that is not going to happen between us. Finally we got off the phone and she again wanted to keep in touch with me but I again declined her offer. My moment to bounce came and I took it because she did not want to take a chance after checking me out through the criminal database online. The bottom line is she now wants to see what she missed.

Note to self and reader be very clear when talking to a past love if one of you gives the wrong impression you may end up in the same situation you originally bounced from. This last story is the ultimate lesson in .

BOUNCE 38

I met this woman through a co-worker. He showed me a picture of her and told me she could not find a decent guy and the last guy she was with tried to separate her from her family.

Little did I know he was performing a service to her but it was viewed as an act of treason by her family? I told my friend to give her my number and she called me and we spoke like old friends. We made plans to go out and stayed out late or what she considered late, something that she never did at least not on a regular basis. His mother called to check on her while we were out she told her we were fine just having a good time. After I returned home we promised to speak again the next day.

I called her the next day and we again spoke for hours. We made plans to go out again but I originally suggested I would cook dinner for her instead of going out. This woman was grown. I mean in her thirties grown and her response to me was rather odd but I figured she was being respectful to her mother. Sometimes people under the control of their parents are a little too respectful to the point they cannot think for themselves.

She told me her mom did not want her going to a man's home that she is not married too. I could not believe what she said but she said it. I didn't make a big deal out of it but I kept it in the back of my mind. The next thing that made me take note of some of the things she and I disagreed on was profanity. I consider myself a grown man on my own for a very long time. Sometimes when I talk I use profanity, nothing too terrible or offensive. When elders or children are around I curb it out of respect or for someone that becomes offended. She and I would take drives and talk. I would use profanity only as an expression not towards her. She never once objected to it or made mention of it. We went on dating and one day I was late picking her up for about five or ten minutes

She came out of the house and announced if I'm going to be late to call her and let her know. I said I was only giving you enough time so you would feel rushed. It has been my experience women tend to require extra time and I ended up waiting on them. I think she could have addressed that a lot better but told her don't be late to anything we are going to attend or I will leave you. She did not like that but I didn't need her verbal browbeating for trying to be considerate. As time went on we passed that milestone and I again was hit with another bombshell. We did start coming to my house to spend time together and she was quite comfortable. She told me she was a virgin and I had no choice but to believe. As our love grew for one another I appreciated her demeanor and candor as we enjoyed one another's company but she would not break her vow to have sex before marriage. One weekend my grandmother happened to be in town and I wanted her to meet the woman I considered asking to marry me.

I told her on the phone during our nightly conversation we were going to my aunt's home where my grandmother was staying so I could introduce her to my grandmother. She agreed and we moved on in our conversation. I called her to tell her I was on my way and was stunned at her response to meeting my grandmother. Apparently after speaking to her mother it was decided she has to take her brother with us to meet my grandmother. I asked her what that was about and she said that's how my mother does things. I told her to forget it and took her the next day without letting her know where we were going. It was a pleasant visit and my grandmother invited us down south for thanksgiving. She promptly told my grandmother my mother will not let me travel with a man I'm not married to. My grandmother gave me the strangest look but did not say anything. After I took her home I returned to my aunt's house to get the feedback. The first thing my grandmother told me was she seems nice but I would not marry that girl. I asked her why and she could not tell me so I chalked it up to no one's good enough stuff. I asked her to marry me and she said yes of course. I was happy she was happy, life was great or so I thought.

The first of many moments to bounce came when I invited her to my jobs Christmas party and she saw my supervisor, a really fine redbone lady who had not too long returned from maternity leave. I was honestly not thinking of this woman in any way other than my boss.

BOUNCE 39

The job was made up of several really cool people and we would go out for drinks or dinner after work maybe once a month. One day my coworkers and I made plans to go to a WWF event now known as the WWE. I asked my fiancée if she wanted to go with us and she declined stating she had to work late. I drove and some others did so my boss and her children rode with me. We all had a great time and I was home by 12am.

I called my soon to be wife the next day and told her all about it. She was less than ecstatic about it and wanted to know why I had to drop my boss off. The next thing I knew she had an attitude about me going out with my coworkers even though she had to work late. I didn't see the relevance in this line of questioning and immediately put all her suspensions to rest. We often walked around and I would see women I knew they looked at me and I looked at them. I never said anything unless they did because women are funny. I did not want to create an awkward situation or a problem where it did not exist.

We spoke about it and she accused me of looking at other women. I eventually left that job and still maintained a good relationship with the people there after all we were still friends. I later made plans for me and my fiancée to attend a WWE event at MSG and informed my fiancée my ex boss asked me to pick up tickets for her and her kids. My fiancée exploded saying "why does she keep hanging around an almost married man."

I called my ex boss and lied. I told her there were no more tickets remaining. I wanted to get my fiancée alone so I could set the record straight. When we arrived I took her engagement ring off her finger and said we are going to get this straight once and for all or we can end it right here and now.

I'm not attracted nor have I ever been to my ex boss if you don't believe me we can leave now and go our separate ways she claimed she believed me. I put the ring back on her finger and we were happy again so I thought.

On Monday I arrived at work and my fiancée's mother called me asking if we could talk because her daughter was unhappy. I was finishing my degree and had class that night and told her it would have to be after class. We met at a nearby McDonald's restaurant around 10pm.

My fiancée arrived with her mom and one of her brothers in tow. Her mother began by saying "I know money has been spent but if you changed your mind we will understand." I replied I did not change my mind. Why do you say so?

Again her mother came out, her face with my daughter was not happy and if you would have done to me what you did to her I would have given you your walking papers.

I looked my fiancée in the face and said if your daughter wants to do that she still can. My fiancée answered me and said no I don't want to call off the wedding.

Her mother said more but I could not tell you what she said at this point because I stopped listening now that I recall it seems her mom did not want her to get married from the jump.

I failed to mention I stopped at home and placed both ring boxes in my jacket in case things went south. I think her mom was hoping I would call it off or become so irate and disrespectful it would be no way she would allow her daughter to marry me.

In retrospect that was my moment to bounce and I let it slip right out of my hands. I truly loved this woman and told myself I could deal with her mom little did I know mom was pulling her daughters string like a puppet. After the discussion all was well in the valley once again. I kissed her good night and went home and did not think about it any further. Several days later I phoned my best friend's mother whom I love like a second mother and told her what happened and she said I should have brought her along I agreed.

We then went on with the plans to get married or should I say she and her mom went on with the wedding plans. She called me to give me an update on the wedding plans. I asked her how far along in the plans are things and she told me they booked a hotel for the wedding and reception.

Then I think she slipped up and told me the food tasting was on Saturday. I asked her what time we have to be there and she said oh my brother is going you don't have to attend.

My mouth dropped to the floor over the phone. I asked her are you marrying me or your brother?" She then said well my parents are paying for everything so they get to make decisions.

I said ok since you want traditional you got it. This was not a moment to bounce but a close one to argue about. We hung up and I had to sit down and catch my breath. I collected myself and got something to drink but remained uneasy about our conversation.

I'm not sure when this occurred but she called me to ask me to finish paying the photographer. I said no you told me your parents were paying for everything because they were traditional so let's be traditional all the way. Needless to say she ended up paying the tab or her traditional mother paid I'm not sure and did not ask. I have an old sense of marriage once married, stay married unless cheating, physical abuse, or ones about to kill the other.

Everyone I know goes through premarital counseling. It's usually a requirement by the minister if you're getting hitched in a church or ceremony. We got together on Friday after work to start our counseling with the minister whose family was old friends of my family. We met with the pastor and were given an assignment to complete by the next meeting which was the following Friday. Our task was to write five things we like and dislike about one another.

It's now the next week she and I never discussed any of our tasks until we arrived back at the church on counseling night. The minister asked her to start with the five things she loved about me and the five she disliked. The first thing out of her mouth was he curses when he talks and sometimes looks at other women. The cursing complaint I'd never heard until that night the woman looking thing I thought we addressed this and put it to bed. The minister observed the look on my face, I'm ready to bounce screw this look on my face. This was the same woman that watched the sopranos on Sunday nights curse from start to finish. She never once turned the television off or changed the channel.

We disagreed that night but the minister quickly squashed my thinking to bounce with some rather encouraging words. I could have come up with a laundry list of things but again my thinking was when you're in love most people overlook the petty things. My only complaint was she harbors things and does not let it go. I was right on point. When we got in the car she asked me where we were going. I answered you are going home. I was still steaming because she ambushed and embarrassed me. I returned home after dropping her off and thought real hard about the events that occurred that evening and others I overlooked. A few days before the big day my fiancée stopped at my house to ask me to do something before or actually during our new start as man and wife.

She asked me after everything was said and done can we have breakfast with her family the next morning before they go back home from out of town and can we drop her mother off home.

She knew I planned to drive us up to the Pocono's for a week after all the fanfare was over because our honeymoon would not be until December after my finals.

I objected and asked her why couldn't one of her brothers or nephew drop her mom home and all of them owned cars. We are starting our new life together and I saw this as a big problem. She became upset and I said ok if we are the last resort then okay. Well the big day finally arrived and we got married. It was a beautiful ceremony and reception.

Remember I told you she was a virgin well I remember her asking me if I'd ever had sex with a virgin a while back before we got married I told her no but I did.

All I can say is that was the easiest entry in virgin history on my wedding night. The next morning we made it down to see her family off mainly because sex was a disaster that night. I asked her to make sure she plans everything around her menstruation and she agreed but to my surprise that night her period started. I'm not one to kiss and talk but there is nothing to talk about since it didn't happen as expected and I never broke the hymen that night. I don't think a starting menstruation makes sex easier for a virgin. I never said a word until now because I was deceived from the start. I was promised by her things would be different after we were married and since we were in our thirties would start a family after we got married. That quickly changed the script and I never saw it coming. We departed the hotel later on our way to the Pocono's for some rest and fun. It was still decent weather and we were just married. When we arrived and unpacked I cooked for us and she started working on something I did not know what it was but she emerged with a page in her hand then I saw she had opened the envelopes she received at the wedding. The next words out of her mouth I have never heard anyone say to their spouse in all my days on earth or even heard from another married couple. She said to me I added up the monetary gifts my guest gave me and what your guest gave you and announced to me you should keep what your guest gave you and I keep what my guest gave me As shocked as I was I agreed to this foolishness only because I trusted my then new bride but deep down I knew we were not going to make it with the this is mine that's yours mentality. We returned home and took most of the gifts we received to her mom's house because our apartment was too small. I believe she was sincere initially but that turned out to be a mistake letting that happen. Our first time out as a married couple with one of her work friends was less than inviting to say the least. I initially refused the invite because I arrived at work at six am and off by two. She did not have to work until nine am off at five. The thing that upset me was she agreed to this dinner knowing I drive to work early in the morning. She committed to telling her friend we would drive her home without discussing it with me. Did I mention her friend lived in New Jersey? I told her before she agreed to me driving anyone home or having dinner let's discuss it first. She became upset and said she would go home to get her car to drive her friend home.

I said fine if that's what you want we later settled that and I drove them home. I tried to make small talk but she did not say much to me during our ride home.

Once we got home that's when the accusations started. She accused me of checking out her friend all night although the friend's boyfriend was at the same table both of them looking at me directly in the face. I always knew I was a bad man but I'm not that bold or stupid.

After that ridiculous disagreement we went to bed the next morning she was gone and she left a note on my computer stating "I need time to think I'm going to my mother's house"

The weekend passed and her birthday was the upcoming Monday. I arranged for flowers, balloons, and a bear graham to arrive at her job before our problems started. She called me at work and thanked me but we got into it again about what happened on Friday night. I told her if you think that's what happened ask your friend to be honest with you and if she agrees I will apologize because that was not my intention. She called me back and said the friend thought we all had a good time. She decided to come home after she realized she misread the situation but I got no apology. She decided to come back home and we celebrated her birthday.

I later found out her friend invited her out to make her feel better after her boss screamed at her, not us. She turned it into a couple invitation at the last minute.

BOUNCE 40

I later found out she was upset because I did not take her out for her birthday. Since I had no idea when she would return I made no plans for us to go out. I did make dinner for her birthday and subsequent return.

We had more disputes over petty nonsense but the kicker came prior to her deciding to bounce. I surprised her with tickets to a play around the holidays. We were both off and no kids yet so it was elementary correct, wrong! If you think I'm being petty listen to this no exaggeration on my behalf. Once I told her the date she said oh I promised my job I would sing with them on that day I don't think I could go. I said I think your job will be to understand your husband wants to spend time with his newlywed wife.

She chose to sing and I went to the play alone. I arrived home and said nothing to her because I was truly disappointed she did not show up. I left her ticket at will call.

I believe the next thing is what set it off. We were in bed one Sunday morning relaxing after some love making. She asked me about going on vacation with her mother and brother.

 I replied don't you think we should take some vacations of our own before we start going on family vacations and besides, we just returned from our honeymoon and I think we should start saving money for a house. She remained silent and said nothing else. I think that's when she hatched the plan to bounce that day.

I will not bore anyone with details but all was good. We were not arguing or fighting. We actually sat on the couch and watched the creature from the black lagoon after I returned from the laundry. She took a shower got dressed, kissed me good-bye and went to her mom's house. This entire episode of my married life can play to K-Solo's your moms in my business the lines goes at the age of 22 you let your mother run your life please feel free to insert the age of your choosing. She arrived home later than usual after going to her mother's house that faithful Sunday morning

I noticed her brother slide in behind her and I knew something was up. She announced to me she was leaving and taking a few things but would return for the rest later. I asked her if there was anything we could discuss. She said no I'm finished talking. I said okay make sure this is a decision you can abide by without question.

She decided to bounce for whatever reason unknown to me and the reason she gave me was ridiculous. Needless to say she went on that vacation with her mom. You know the sad bride and all. If anyone reading this book cannot decipher what really happened read it again or have someone explain it to you. In case you're wondering she tried to return to me several times and we even spoke a few times but as long as her mom ran her life we had no chance. I could not in good conscience return to that situation. We both have since moved on with our lives and I'm very happy. I've met plenty of mothers, some nosy, mean, nasty, pleasant and some that allow their daughters to live their own lives.

Note to self and reader advice to anyone and its only advice when you encounter a resistant mother and the woman is grown I mean over thirty grown and she is still under the thumb of her mother and this applies to men of the same age run as fast as you can. If one is not grown enough to make decisions concerning their future and have to run to mommy instead of dealing with the issues with the person they plan on sharing a life with it's a recipe for disaster take it from me. Usually the parents of these people are bitter and unhappy with how their lives turned out and do not want to see their children do better than they did in life. I don't know if it's intentional or subliminal but that type of thinking wreaks havoc on the adult children's lives.

Note to self don't ever repeat that mistake again!!!!!!!!!

www.ingramcontent.com/pod-product-compliance
Lightning Source LLC
LaVergne TN
LVHW091559060526
838200LV00036B/917